WINNING THE FATHERHOOD GAME

A Playbook for the Five Scores that Matter

J. SHANNON EADS

Winning the Fatherhood Game

Published in association with Ivey Beckman Enterprises.
www.iveyharringtonbeckman.com

Some names in this book have been changed to protect privacy.

Printed in the United States of America
ISBN 978-0-578-33523-0

This book is dedicated to my sons, Tyler and Jase.
I'm so blessed that you call me Dad.
I pray that the words I've written
will guide you when I'm around and when I'm not.

Acknowledgments

I want to thank my dad and mom, Jerry and Judy Eads, for being great parents. Because you guided me with wisdom, I'm able to coach Tyler and Jase.

Tim and Linda O'Keefe, you raised an amazing daughter. I'm blessed to share life with Michelle.

Michelle, you're a beautiful wife and mom. Going through life with you is the dream of a lifetime. I'm a better man because of you.

I want to thank my brother, Shane Eads, and my brothers-in-law, Allan and Charles O'Keefe, for standing by me through thick and thin.

Jon Duncan, Keith Cureton, and John Baird, you three always make time for me. Thank you for listening to both my victories and my struggles.

Bob Davis, Keith Herr, Danny Shill, John Coon, Ken Maroney, Bryan Cannon, Rich Lazarra, and Jeff Conyers, your friendship means the world to me. You prove that men are stronger when we do life together.

I want to thank all the members of Browning Road Baptist Church for surrounding me with wisdom and support. You are living examples of God's mission for the church.

Ivey Harrington Beckman, thank you for everything you did to help me complete *Winning the Fatherhood Game*. Your editing skills brought my words to life.

The Fatherhood Anthem

"The one who lives under the protection of the Most High dwells in the shadow of the Almighty." (Psalm 91:1)

Contents

SECTION 1

VALUE THE WARMUP

Understand the Importance of Keeping Score

Fatherhood requires a serious game plan. As a father, the lives of your children and others under your influence depend on you playing the Fatherhood Game with your whole heart. Are you in it to win it?

Some men shirk fatherhood, and children whose fathers drop the ball can experience debilitating injuries with lifelong consequences. Maybe you know this first hand because your father dropped the game ball—or never picked it up.

But your father's failure doesn't mean you can't be a winning dad who raises champions. You can change your life and those of children you love when you go all-in for the Fatherhood Game.

You see, godly fatherhood begins in the heart muscle. **If you've given your heart to Jesus Christ, you're already on the winning team.** I like to think of Psalm 91:1 as the anthem that reverberates in the soul of a dad who has committed his heart, soul, mind, and strength to win the Fatherhood Game:

> "*The one who lives under the protection of the Most High dwells in the shadow of the Almighty.*"

Those words confirm that God has your back, and He wants you to move forward to make a difference in the lives of the children under your influence. Aligning yourself with God is the ultimate game-changer, the winning edge you need to raise children who are champions.

How to Gain the Winning Edge

When my wife, Michelle, and I first began to take our son, Tyler to the Tampa Bay Rays games, I would always spot the individuals keeping the scorebooks. Those scorekeepers were diligent and never missed a play. At first, I thought they were missing out on the game, but I soon realized they viewed it with a strategic lens. While I was watching for a win, they tracked every aspect of the game to guide improvements for their team and individual players.

My family would leave those games with fun memories, but the scorekeepers departed with treasure troves of data: stolen bases, walks, hits, strikeouts, and homeruns. They scored the game with ball counts, pitcher and batter stats, unforced errors, stolen bases, and winning lineups—all golden elements for coaching players to improve.

You see, scorekeepers know that ignorance never gets credit for a win. Knowledge is power, and understanding God's plan for you as a man and the rules and nuances of the Fatherhood Game can make you a winner.

When my older brother, Shane, and I started playing ball, parents were forced, tricked, begged, or even bribed into keeping the scorebook. The coach had an old green army bag from his military days. It contained bats, catching gear, used and new balls, and the dreaded scorebook. Parents often came late to the game just to avoid getting anywhere near that green bag.

In hindsight, those reluctant parents missed out big time on helping their children gain the winning edge as players. Keeping score seemed tedious to them. Instead of gleaning facts and stats to improve their children's game skills and mindsets, they preferred to view the game (and shout displeasure) from a distance.

Sadly, the hesitancy of those parents to engage in game scorekeeping is also true of many fathers these days. Many watch their children as bleacher-seat spectators of the Fatherhood Game instead of being in it to win it. **But becoming scorekeepers as men and fathers is how we succeed in life and coach our children to become champions.** When you find yourself trying to wing it as a father, recall the wisdom of 2 Timothy 2.

> "*You, therefore, my son, be strong in the grace that is in Christ Jesus. And what you have heard from me in the presence of many witnesses, commit to faithful men who will be able to teach others also.*" (2 Timothy 2:1-2)

> "*Also, if anyone competes as an athlete, he is not crowned unless he competes according to the rules.*" (2 Timothy 2:5)

Learn the Playbook

Winning the Fatherhood Game is a straightforward playbook for training you to become an intentional scorekeeper who focuses on the Five Vital Scores that matter in life—and a father who coaches children to concentrate on them too. The next section of *Winning the Fatherhood Game* will provide a muscle-building training regime for each of the Five Vital Scores. Here's a summary of those scores.

#1 Your Past Score: Acknowledge It.

To become a winner as a man and father, you must review the game tape of the hard-fought victories in your life, along with the disappointments, failures, and heartbreaks that can hamstring you from being fully engaged in becoming the person God wants you to be.

Scripture should be the heartbeat of your playbook as you assess your Past Score. Through the power of the Holy Spirit working in your life, **Scripture will ground your feet in truth while focusing your eyes on**

your higher calling as a son of God and a father to the children you love.

Here are three robust, forward-thinking Scripture verses that will build your muscle and momentum as you assess your Past Score in the next section of this playbook. Commit these verses to memory by posting them on the mirror where you shave every morning. Recite them before your head out the door.

> "*Not that I have already reached the goal or am already fully mature, but I make every effort to take hold of it because I also have been taken hold of by Christ Jesus. Brothers, I do not consider myself to have taken hold of it. But one thing I do: Forgetting what is behind and reaching forward to what is ahead, I pursue as my goal the prize promised by God's heavenly call in Christ Jesus.*" (Philippians 3:12-14)

#2 Your Present Score: Assess It.

Your goal is to create a God-empowered game plan that establishes the sweat equity required today to move beyond your Past Score toward His purpose for your life. This game-planning requires positive thinking empowered by God's hand on your life. Just as repetitive drills enable special-team players to complete plays with accuracy and agility, daily time in Scripture bolsters your game plan.

Colossians 3:23 is a powerful verse to memorize as your daily pep-talk for developing a positive, God-focused spirit, along with the tough mental mindset you need to win the Fatherhood Game.

"*Whatever you do, do it enthusiastically, as something done for the Lord and not for men.*" (Colossians 3:23)

Post this verse where you will see it repeatedly throughout your day—near the gear shift of your vehicle, on your desk, as the screen-saver image on your cell phone. Think of it as the coach who gets in your face to keep you thinking straight as you assess your Present Score in the pages ahead.

#3 Your Potential Score: Aspire to It.

Empowered by a hands-on relationship with God, you can live your best life as a man and a father. Believe that because it's true. God-empowered self-confidence changes the game. **The fact that you don't have to play the Fatherhood Game solo is the grip you need to overcome crippling fear about being a strong man and a godly father.**

In the next section of this playbook, you'll receive more training for your Potential Score. To begin, memorize Isaiah 41:10 as your shin guard verse. Repeat it to yourself anytime fear and doubt attempt to kick your legs out from under you as you run toward your Potential Score. Write it on your baseball bat, your basketball, or post it in a place where you often encounter resistance to achieving your goal of becoming the best man and father possible.

> "*Do not fear, for I am with you: do not be afraid, for I am your God. I will strengthen you; I will help; I will hold on to you with My righteous right hand.*" (Isaiah 41:10)

#4 Your Permanent Score: Affirm It.

Lock your heart on the endgame because your Permanent Score—where you spend eternity—is the most important score of all. In the next section of this playbook, you'll receive intense coaching on affirming your Permanent Score, but here's the core truth: One day, the final whistle will blow on your life. After that, it's game over on Earth. The two choices for your eternity couldn't be more divergent:

- *victorious, full-breath life in heaven*
- *or a devastating, unredeemable loss in hell, forever separated from God and anything and anyone you love.*

God's Ultimate Game Plan placed His sinless Son, Jesus Christ, on a cross to sacrifice everything so you could win that victorious, full-breath life in heaven. Securing your Permanent Score in heaven doesn't require intense study or a work-focused routine. Instead, it's a simple act of repentance and faith:

> "*For you are saved by grace through faith, and this is not from yourselves; it is God's gift—not from works, so that no one can boast.* (Ephesians 2:8-9)

> "*For God loved the world in this way: He gave His One and Only Son, so that everyone who believes in Him will not perish but have eternal life.*" (John 3:16)

#5 Your Perfect Score: Achieve It.

Throughout all time, only Jesus lived a perfect life on Earth. If you place your trust in Him as your Savior, you, too, will achieve perfection.

But you'll have to wait for it. You'll achieve your Perfect Score only after you ditch your banged-up body and enter heaven. Meanwhile, your body, mind, and spirit will take hard knocks. There will be bruises, blood, broken bones, wounded hearts. And pain. Lots of pain. You'll make mistakes and likely suffer for them. Perfection is not possible on this third rock from the sun.

You'll learn more about your Perfect Score in the next section of this playbook. But on those days when everything seems to go wrong, and you feel like the most fallible person on the planet, make sure you've committed Philippians 3:21 and 4:13 to memory. These verses can serve as shots of adrenaline to get your weary, banged-up human body up and moving toward a muscular eternal mindset.

> *"He will transform the body of our humble condition into the likeness of His glorious body, by the power that enables Him to subject everything to Himself."* (Philippians 3:21)

> *"I am able to do all things through Him who strengthens me."* (Philippians 4:13)

Now that you understand the **Five Vital Scores,** the importance of keeping score in the Fatherhood Game, and the discipline that requires, it's time to charge forward with a winning game plan, empowered by the power of God and the truths of Scripture.

> *"For I know the plans I have for you," this is the Lord's declaration, "plans for your welfare , not for disaster, to give you hope and a future."* (Jeremiah 29:11)

Envision Your Winning Game Plan

As the father of two boys, I want to model a game plan that exudes the values of the **Five Vital Scores.** In 2020—a challenging year for everyone—I discovered I had stage-three cancer. My game plan is in high gear these days. I'm fully engaged as a father—living for a cancer cure while coaching my sons, Tyler and Jase, with increased intensity. I want to ensure they're equipped to play hard and dream big with God. I want them to embrace eternity with confidence and gusto.

Don't you want that for the children you love?

Tim Tebow delivered "The Promise" speech after a gut-wrenching 31-30 loss to Ole Miss on September 27, 2008. It created a winning game plan for life:

"*To the fans and everybody in Gator Nation, I'm sorry, extremely sorry. We were hoping for an undefeated season. That was my goal, something Florida's never done here. But I promise you one thing, a lot of good will come out of this. You will never see any player in the entire country play as hard as I will play the rest of the season, and you will never see someone push the rest of the team as hard as I will push everybody the rest of the season, and you will never see a team play harder than we will the rest of the season. God bless.*"[1]

Tebow came to grips with that loss to Ole Miss, but he refused to let the past define or confine him—or his team. Instead, he studied that game tape for hours on end to create a plan to move forward.

Tebow's game strategy for the remainder of the 2008 season was straightforward:

- ✓ **He assessed his past failures and disappointments.**
- ✓ **He owned the sweat work his present life required.**
- ✓ **He believed in his potential.**
- ✓ **He locked his heart on the end game, placing his future in God's hands.**
- ✓ **He understood that he could not achieve perfection on Earth but pressed on with purpose, empowered by a higher calling.**

Tebow followed through on his promise—leading the Florida Gators on a 10-game winning streak, seizing the SEC championship from the vice-like grip of the Alabama Crimson Tide, and capping the memorable season by winning the National Championship.

A lot of good did come from that gut-wrenching loss to Ole Miss. **And a lot of good can come from your losses and those of children you love.**

Vince Lombardi, one of the most winning coaches of all time, understood the freedom found in a God-focused, Holy Spirit-empowered game plan:

"When we place our dependence in God, we are unencumbered, and we have no worry. In fact, we may even be reckless, insofar as our part in the production is concerned. This confidence, this sureness of action, is both contagious and an aid to the perfect action. The rest is in the hands of God – and this is the same God, gentlemen, who has won all His battles up to now." [2]

You become a better man (and a winning father who can coach younger generations to become champions) when you:

- ✓ **acknowledge your past disappointments and mistakes,**
- ✓ **assess the hard work your present circumstances require,**
- ✓ **believe in your potential,**
- ✓ **focus on a future that embraces God's plan and purpose for your life,**
- ✓ **strive not for perfection but a purpose-driven life.**

The promise of Proverbs 13:20 is championship coaching for men who choose to go all-in for the Fatherhood Game. Memorize it and repeat it to yourself daily as a helmet for safety and wisdom.

"The one who walks with the wise will become wise, but a companion of fools will suffer harm." (Proverbs 13:20)

Always remember that Fatherhood scorekeeping is not compiled in numbers and trophies but rather in helping yourself and others cross the finish line of life on Earth with a victorious Permanent Score in eternity.

With that in mind, section two of this playbook includes:

- ✓ **stories of real men who chose to get in the game,**
- ✓ **fatherhood tips ("The Dad Huddle"),**
- ✓ **self-assessment tools for tracking progress ("Scorecard").**

Now that you're warmed up, take the field. There's an important game to win—The Fatherhood Game.

The Dad Huddle

God chose me to father my sons. He chose you to father your children. Being present in their daily lives is the first step toward winning the Fatherhood Game.

So get out of the bleachers and in the game. Sure, you'll make mistakes. I've certainly made my share; all fathers do. But you'll do a lot of things right. Be yourself and trust God along the way.

A child wants a dad who is present, not perfect. A dirty game jersey means you're playing hard to win.

Scorecard – Your Warmup Self-assessment

1. List the five scores that matter in the Fatherhood Game
   -
   -
   -
   -
   -

3. Which score do you anticipate will be the most challenging for you?

4. Where would you say you are as a father?

   ☐ In the Fatherhood Game with grass stains on my jersey
   ☐ Warming the bench
   ☐ In the locker room, trying to suit up
   ☐ Not yet in the ballpark

5. Is there anything hamstringing you from placing your life, and the lives of your children, in God's hands? If so, note that here and ask God to help you heal so you can move forward in the Fatherhood Game.

SECTION 2
OWN YOUR FIVE VITAL SCORES

#1

YOUR PAST SCORE: ACKNOWLEDGE IT

You must review your game tape.

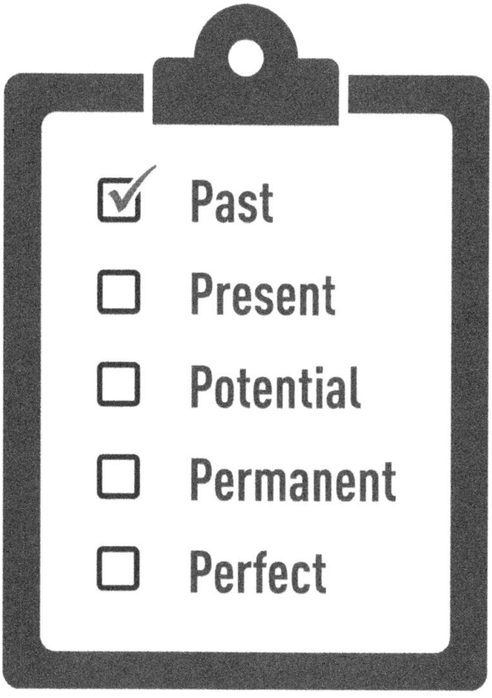

Push Past the Pain

We cringe when we watch the graphic videos of athletes career-threatening injuries. And yet, many athletes have overcome their gruesome injuries to return to the game and play heroically. Think of Tiger Woods, who entered the 2008 U.S. Open after suffering a double stress fracture of his left tibia. Woods gritted through the pain for five days and 91 holes to defeat Rocco Mediate in a playoff. That 2008 championship win is legendary.[3] And on April 14, 2019, despite other injuries and setbacks that threatened his career, Woods again played on to win the Masters Tournament for the fifth time.[4]

Then there's Giancarlo Stanton. An 80-mile-an-hour pitch slammed into his face during a game with the Milwaukee Brewers in the 2014 season. The impact caused facial fractures, lacerations, and dental damage. Such a heater might have left other players heading for the gates permanently. But not Stanton. The Miami Marlin slugger returned the next season to hit 27 home runs.[5]

Pushing past the pain to win is part of sports. And part of life.

So, it's time to review your game tape. Where did you score some victories? Where have you been hit? What's fractured? Where has failure knocked the wind out of you? You must deal with the impact of past pain in your life because it can stifle your Present and Potential Scores, just as a torn ACL can cripple a running back.

For many men, past pain has left them out of the Fatherhood Game and far from the life score God has planned. Those traumas can also wound their children, stifling them from reaching their full potential.

The pain that changed my life hit me like an 80-mile-an-hour curveball. I wish I could ask that man why he abused a struggling student who needed tutoring—a kid who needed help, not harm—but he died many years ago. That individual used a lot of mind games to keep me silent, which is common with abusers. However, I want other men to know that facing my pain head-on made me a winner—and someone who can connect with others who have painful Past Scores.

I pushed through my pain and shame, not by self-medicating or self-destructing, but by forgiving a man who didn't deserve an ounce of forgiveness. For years I wanted him to suffer and then suffer some more. However, God, in His timing, showed me that only grace could heal my wounds. Anger had done nothing for me. And anger will not help you.

As hard as it was to accept, I had to forgive that man. I accomplished that feat with God's amazing grace, which beats any painkiller on the market. **Rather than run from my pain and God, I chose to run to Him.** I reviewed my gut-wrenching game tape and faced down that pain to allow myself to win in life. It wasn't easy, but, man, did it make me feel like a winner.

God's grace and forgiveness empowered me to forgive that man. And that forgiveness catapulted me out of a dark place where I was stuck for a long time. Like Tim Tebow, as a result of moving forward from my Past Score, I'm now able to win big in my life.

Colossians 1:13-14 is an invigorating Scripture to memorize and recite when you're assessing anything that might have cast darkness on your Past Score. Forgiveness, my friend, is powerful stuff.

"*He has rescued us from the domain of darkness and transferred us into the kingdom of the Son He loves. We have redemption, the forgiveness of sins, in Him.*" (Colossians 1:13-14)

New Beginnings

My friend, Ben Drennen, was walloped as a kid too. He lived his childhood as a victim of his dad's duality, often asking himself, *In which state of being—drunk or sober—is the true nature of a binge drinker revealed? Is it the sober father who supports you when you're down or the drunken father who verbally abuses you?*

That uncertainty led Ben to question his worth, burdened him with guilt, shackled him with shame, and crippled him with anxiety. Despite all that, he excelled in school and became a believer at age 18. However, in college, like many children of alcoholics, Ben began to walk the path of his father, binge drinking to the point of regular blackouts. After college, his drinking intensified.

Of those days Ben recalls, "The irony of it all is that the side effects of my own drinking were identical to the effects my father's drinking had on me. It led me to feel worthless. It burdened me with guilt, shackled me with shame, and crippled me with anxiety. How Satan must have reveled in my turmoil! I felt an utter sense of nothingness and the weight of the world all at once. I was stuck in neutral—ruminating over the past and wasting my future."

At one point, Ben begged God to take the urge to drink away from him.

"I wanted Him to do that for me," he confessed. "I wanted the easy out, the immediate healing. How spiritually lazy I was!"

After a long drinking binge, Ben's family found him passed out in his truck one morning. It was humiliating and eye-opening.

"Through the pain of a brain-bending hangover, I realized that if I wanted to stop drinking, I had to add action to my prayers," Ben admitted. "With a shaky hand, I put down the bottle, and day by day, God steadied me and moved mountains in my life.

"Now, I'm no longer a prisoner of my past—all that guilt, shame, and anxiety that held me back. My life is worth something again. Dealing with the past was the change I had to make in my life before I could begin anew."

Like many men with painful Past Scores, Ben embraced the new-beginnings truth of Isaiah 43:19. It's a visionary verse to memorize because God shines a bright and steady light toward the future through it. Post it where you can absorb its light every day!

"Look, I am about to do something new;
even now it is coming. Do you not see it?
Indeed, I will make a way in the wilderness,
rivers in the desert." (Isaiah 43:19)

How's that for a power shot! **God's Word beats any temporary chemical boost on the market because its sustenance is life-changing and eternal.**

Failure as Fuel

In May of 2021, Phil Mickelson, 50, won the PGA Championship to become the oldest major champion in golf history. How did he achieve this? By using failure as the fuel to drive him to work harder. Some might argue that no pro player in history has been written off more often than Mickelson.

> *"I've failed many times in my life and career and because of this I've learned a lot. Instead of feeling defeated countless times, I've used it as fuel to drive me to work harder. So today, join me in accepting our failures. Let's use them to motivate us to work even harder."* [6]

As difficult as it might seem after multiple failures and setbacks, don't count yourself out. And **don't allow others to count you out as a man or a father. Because God most certainly hasn't.**

Trust God with a Past Score that may have made you feel like a loser all your life. Utilize the power of forgiveness. Like Ben, put action to your prayers. Use past failures as fuel. Find the courage to sweat through the activity that allows God to heal your past. Draw on the power of the Holy Spirit to keep you moving in the right direction.

Like Mickelson, today is a great day to use the fuel of failure to propel you forward from your Past Score. Winston Churchill once said, "Success is walking from failure to failure with no loss of enthusiasm."[7] So, get enthused about making some positive changes in your life.

Are you ready to work harder through the power of the Holy Spirit? God promises that, together, you make a great team!

> *"But you will receive power when the Holy Spirit has come on you, and you will be My witnesses in Jerusalem, in all Judea and Samaria, and to the ends of the earth."* (Act 1:8)

> *"In the same way the Spirit also joins to help in our weakness, because we do not know what to pray for as we should, but the Spirit Himself intercedes for us with unspoken groanings. And He who searches the hearts knows the Spirit's mind-set, because He intercedes for the saints according to the will of God."*
> *(Romans 8:26-27)*

Your Past Score doesn't have to define or confine you! Use it as a launching pad for the new things God wants to do in your life. With God by your side, you can hit life out of the park, no matter what inning you're in.

> *"Be strong and courageous; don't be terrified or afraid of them. For it is the Lord your God who goes with you; He will not leave you or forsake you."* (Deuteronomy 31:6)

Prove to yourself and your children that you've got this. Stand up, deal with your past, and lean into your future with the Heisman trophy stance. It's a winner, and so are you.

The Dad Huddle

My boys and I enjoy watching sports together. We've talked about victories won because coaches and players took the time to watch opponents' game tapes to spot strengths and weaknesses.

Invest the time to overcome a past that hinders your ability to be a winning dad today. Show your children how to live in the present with nothing holding them back.

Scorecard – You Past Score Self-assessment

1. If there's an open wound from your past that continues to hold you back, face it head-on as your first step toward winning the Fatherhood Game. Identify your level of hurt, with ten being the most severe.

   1 2 3 4 5 6 7 8 9 10

2. Forgiving someone doesn't mean you have to bring them into your present world if that would risk more pain. However, forgiveness can release you to a fresh beginning.

   Identify where you are in the process of forgiving someone (with one signaling, "Man, I'm stuck in a ditch about this," and ten signaling, "It wasn't easy, but I've forgiven this person and moved forward with my life).

   1 2 3 4 5 6 7 8 9 10

3. A counselor, pastor, or godly friend can help you healthily review your game tape. When you're committed to healing from the past, you'll invest time and effort into it. How aggressively are you taking this step?

   1 2 3 4 5 6 7 8 9 10

4. It's essential to acknowledge breakthroughs from your past. Have you, a counselor, a friend, or family members noticed a positive change in you? Record your breakthrough level below.

   1 2 3 4 5 6 7 8 9 10

5. How have your breakthroughs changed your life to this point?

6. How ready are you to exit the confining dugout of your past, grip the bat, and swing for the future in the Fatherhood Game?

1 2 3 4 5 6 7 8 9 10

6. What weaknesses did your father pass on that you need to correct?

7. What strengths did he give you that can propel you forward?

8. What do you wish someone had done for you as a child that you can now do for your children or others?

#2

YOUR PRESENT SCORE: ASSESS IT

Because the ball is in your hands.

Your River of Sweat

Nick Saban, the most successful college football coach of his generation, can often be seen chewing out a Crimson Tide player for a busted play. Saban always has the endgame in mind, but he is ever aware of the Present Score.

Saban wants the best for his players, so he demands the best of them. He'll turn around a disappointing game score with intense and intentional drills on the practice field. Remember the stunning pick-six fiasco of the 2013 Iron Bowl? Alabama's loss to Auburn in those last seconds led to a lot of sweat-inducing special-teams drills. If someone were to drain the turf on the Crimson Tide practice field of players' sweat, a river would flow through the University of Alabama campus.

Saban summed up his Present Score philosophy in three sentences.

> **"What happened yesterday is history.**
> **What happens tomorrow is a mystery.**
> **What we do today makes a difference."** [8]

Vijay Singh is a professional golfer from Fiji. Early on, Vijay had a unique ritual. Following each round of golf he played, he would go to the driving range and hit balls for hours. Vijay knew he needed to practice today to improve his past round of golf and arrive at his best score tomorrow. His motto? "Get after it."

So, my friend, it's time for you to get after it. What you do today makes a difference.

Today is the day to assess your Present Score.

Today is the day to begin doing the things that will make a difference tomorrow in your life and the lives of the children you love.

It's time to demand the best of yourself.

It's time to create a sweat-river of your own.

You're on the field now. Listen to the coaching of Philippians 3:13-14, which signals that you have reconciled your Past Score and are willing to do the work necessary today to achieve a Present Score that honors God.

> *"Brothers, I do not consider myself to have taken hold of it. But one thing I do: Forgetting what is behind and reaching forward to what is ahead, I pursue as my goal the prize promised by God's heavenly call in Christ Jesus."* (*Philippians* 3:13-14)

And remember, you're not on the Fatherhood Game field alone. It's time to pursue the big goal. Approach today with confidence, knowing that God is your constant ally. He believes in you, so believe in yourself.

> *"Search for the Lord and for His strength; seek His face always."* (1 Chronicles 16:11)

> *"I am sure of this, that He who started a good work in you will carry it on to completion until the day of Christ Jesus."* (*Philippians* 1:6)

The Opportunity of Difficulty

One day the starting date and ending date of your life will be etched on your headstone. You cannot control those dates, but you can control the dash that separates them. That dash is powerful—and it's yours to live. Of course, no one ever said living the dash is easy, but as Albert Einstein explained, "In the middle of difficulty lies opportunity."[9]

My friend Tim Jennings knows full well the pain and difficulty of the dash. After sixteen years of marriage, his wife filed for divorce to figure out who she wanted to be other than Tim's wife. It was a blindsiding hit that threw him to the turf. Tim was suddenly a single father in his forties.

"I felt robbed. Half my material possessions were gone," Tim recalled. "But the worst part was the parental sharing agreement. On the days I had to drop off the kids, the pain was excruciating. Instead of the excitement of laughter, energy, and hugs when I got home, there was dead silence."

Tim could have thrown in the towel and given up. His present circumstances were not at all what he expected or wanted. Tim could have filled that silent house with the voice of another woman or numbed the pain with alcohol or drugs. He could have worked more so he didn't have as much time to think about what he had lost. He could have chosen to walk off the fatherhood field altogether and live his life by his own rules.

Instead, Tim chose to create a sweat river of his own by running the drills that would change his Present Score and give his children the best opportunity to become lifelong champions.

"I knew that if I stood still, I wouldn't last," Tim recalled. "I had to run and run hard. I had to get after it. I needed to run to God so that all my pain wouldn't return void. As difficult as my circumstances were, God promises me in Scripture that He loves me and wants what's best for me. His promises are unchanging."

Tim went on to say, "God's Word became more tangible for me than the shirt on my back. My life had changed in an instant, and I needed something unchanging; I needed someone I could count on, someone to put my faith in so I could finish the race."

Like daily pushups, Tim recited Isaiah 26:3 time and time again to get through the sleepless nights:

> *"You will keep the mind that is dependent on You in perfect peace, for it is trusting in You."* (Isaiah 26:3)

That steadfastness of mind and grounded trust empowered Tim to stay consistent with his children, bringing much-needed physical, emotional, and spiritual equilibrium back into their lives—packing lunches, participating in school functions, doing homework, attending church.

When Tim felt exhausted, others poured into him like Gatorade.®

"I encountered so many individuals who had just the right word for me at the right time," Tim recalled with gratitude.

A lot of blood, sweat, tears, and years later, Tim has discovered that thankfulness defeats bitterness in every situation. It changes the game.

"When you can see things from the side of the thankful field, you can be patient with God and realize that He truly is working all things out for His glory," Tim explained.

"Over a decade away from a time when I felt like something had died inside of me, I can honestly say God's guidance and unending concern for my life have always been at work. He's been helping me raise my children every breath of the way.

"I tell them, *Don't ever wish time away, even when it's a hard time. Instead, look up and thank God for the sweat of every day because it's helping you reach your full potential for God's glory.*"

Tim's advice to his children mirrors Romans 8:18:

> *"For I consider that the sufferings of this present time are not worth comparing with the glory that is going to be revealed to us."* (Romans 8:18)

Your Time Out is Over

Weeks before I was diagnosed with cancer, I lost a job I loved. It felt like an unseen, hot-tempered referee had called a harsh timeout.

Because of COVID, employment was limited, so I began to work for a restoration company part-time, refurbishing old apartments.

As I worked, I started asking God to point me to individuals I could recruit to minister to the residents of those apartments.

I called churches and pastors in the area. No results. *Why?* Because God wasn't asking them to minister to the people in those apartments. Instead, He was telling me that my time out was over, and He expected me to be fully present right where I was. **On the backside of a run-down apartment building, I heard God say, "Shannon, this is why I brought you here today. This apartment complex is your present, and I want you to score here."**

Later that day, a young boy with a beautiful smile walked out of his apartment and asked if I would play ball with him. We talked as we threw a ball, and he never stopped smiling. The whole time I was with him, God's peace was falling all over me. And I heard God whisper, "*Shannon, your time out is over. Pour into these kids.*"

Like me, you've had some busted plays in the past. Regardless of what may have you sitting on the bench, your time out is over, too, my friend. Get back in the game and work up a sweat. Distance yourself from anyone or anything that can hinder your ability to succeed today. Adopt Nick Saban's philosophy about your current score:

> "*What happened yesterday is history.*
> *What happens tomorrow is a mystery.*
> *What we do today makes a difference.*"

The ball is in your hands, and it's time for you to run!

Practice Today for the Win Tomorrow

My son Tyler and I play golf together these days. He quickly embraced the discipline of practicing his swing. I've watched Tyler stick with it, sand trap after sand trap, triple bogey after triple bogey. Undeterred, he keeps at it. Show me someone willing to make the sacrifice of practice, and I will show you someone ready to win.

Michael Jordan once said, "Champions do not become champions when they win an event, but in the hours, weeks, months, and years they spend preparing for it. The victorious performance itself is merely a demonstration of their championship character."[10]

My son is developing a championship character every time he swings a club. His eyes and heart are on the long game, and that gets him past the bogeys.

Philippians 4:8-9 is not just food for thought; it's breakfast, lunch, and dinner for champions.

> *"Finally brothers, whatever is true, whatever is honorable, whatever is just, whatever is pure, whatever is lovely, whatever is commendable—if there is any moral excellence and if there is any praise—dwell on these things. Do what you have learned and received and heard and seen in me, and the God of peace will be with you."* (Philippians 4:8-9)

Are you developing your championship character as you take your swings at life each day? What's getting you past bogeys and sand traps? In the Fatherhood Game, practicing today is what connects the hardships to success tomorrow.

As you go through life, you'll find it much easier to postpone much-needed fatherhood practice. These days, you might see every excuse to delay playing the Fatherhood Game. But delaying is just the first step toward quitting. So keep swinging, my friend. Keep developing the muscle of a championship character. Your children depend on it.

For dads, Luke 21:19 is worthy of megaphone volume:

> *"By your endurance gain your lives."* (Luke 21:19)

When you commit daily to doing what it takes to develop your character, you lead your children by example. You endure to gain life, and through your example, your children learn how to endure to triumph in their lives.

Help the children under your influence memorize 1 Corinthians 15:58 so they, like you, can say it aloud when the going gets tough:

> "*Therefore, my dear brothers, be steadfast, immovable, always excelling in the Lord's work, knowing that your labor in the Lord is not in vain.*" (1 Corinthians 15:58)

Vince Lombardi nailed character development when he said:

> "*The difference between a successful person and others is not a lack of strength, a lack of knowledge, but rather a lack of will. Mental toughness is many things and rather difficult to explain. Its qualities are sacrifice and self-denial. Also, most importantly, it is combined with a perfectly disciplined will that refuses to give in. It's a state of mind. You could call it 'character in action.'*"[11]

Does your state of mind today exude character in action? Refuse to give in or give up, especially when the Fatherhood Game gets hard, long, and muddy.

Ephesians 2:10 bolsters fathers of faith best because it focuses on the Who behind the disciplined *will* of present-day character building:

> "*For we are His creation, created in Christ Jesus for good works,*
> *which God prepared ahead of time*
> *so that we should walk in them.*" (Ephesians 2:10)

Work Harder

As a youth, if you never found yourself in the awkward position of being picked for teams, consider yourself blessed and sheltered.

When I was a kid, team members were chosen by captains, usually the two oldest kids. No one wanted to be the last one picked. I was the last kid a couple of times, and it still burns to this day.

But those humiliating days didn't break me. I didn't toss down my glove and walk away. Instead, I decided to play harder. The team captains may not have viewed me as a winner, but I did—so I stuck it out!

Derek Jeter got the soul of determined work ethic right when he said, "There may be people who have more talent than you. But there's no excuse for anyone to work harder than you do." [12]

When we fathers add faith to a determined work ethic, things get powerful. Ephesians 3:20 is the pep talk all dads need on those bad days when things don't go our way, and we get picked last—or not at all.

> *Now to Him who is able to do above and beyond all that we ask or think according to the power that works in us."* (Ephesians 3:20)

With Christ, you have incredible power within you to build onward and upward. **Grow from the mistakes you make as a dad. Learn from disappointments. Just do not quit. Never, ever quit.**

The Fatherhood Game Plan hasn't changed. It's been in place for a long time, my friend, and it's a good one. Keep playing hard every day to improve your Present Score. And through God's strength and steadfastness, you can do it when you refuse to quit and put strong character into action each day.

The Dad Huddle

Dads, it's challenging to be an aggressive player without hearing an occasional whistle. Simple fouls are a part of life, but fouling out of the game as a dad isn't an option. We dads must stay in it to win it! Sure, we'll make mistakes because we still have the "old man" in us even when we know Jesus as Savior. We cannot achieve perfection apart from a relationship with Jesus. But the past is the past, and those fouls need to stay in the past. Forgive yourself, forgive others, and lean in for the win today.

Scorecard—Your Present Score Self-assessment

1. Identify any people, places, or products that continue to affect your present life negatively.

    -
    -
    -

2. What steps are you taking to distance yourself from these obstacles?

3. What healthy fillers have you chosen to replace negative distractions?

4. What two things will you do this week to get back in the Fatherhood Game after a time out?

5. Assess your Present Score progress in the following areas:

    Faith: You're taking steps to mature your faith through Bible study and prayer. (The higher number denotes intensity.)

    1 2 3 4 5 6 7 8 9 10

    Family: You're working toward growing closer to your family members.

    1 2 3 4 5 6 7 8 9 10

Friends: You're developing strong relationships with godly men.

1 2 3 4 5 6 7 8 9 10

Finances: You're taking steps to manage your money well.

1 2 3 4 5 6 7 8 9 10

Employment: You're happy with your job, or are you taking steps to find one that fulfills you.

1 2 3 4 5 6 7 8 9 10

Fun/Exercise: You're taking steps toward living a healthy life-style—taking time off for fun, exercising, and eating well.

1 2 3 4 5 6 7 8 9 10

Focus: You're focused on modeling a good work ethic for your children

1 2 3 4 5 6 7 8 9 10

Flexibility/forgiveness: You're able to adapt to change and are working toward forgiving others.

1 2 3 4 5 6 7 8 9 10

#3

YOUR POTENTIAL SCORE: ASPIRE TO IT

Do you believe in yourself?

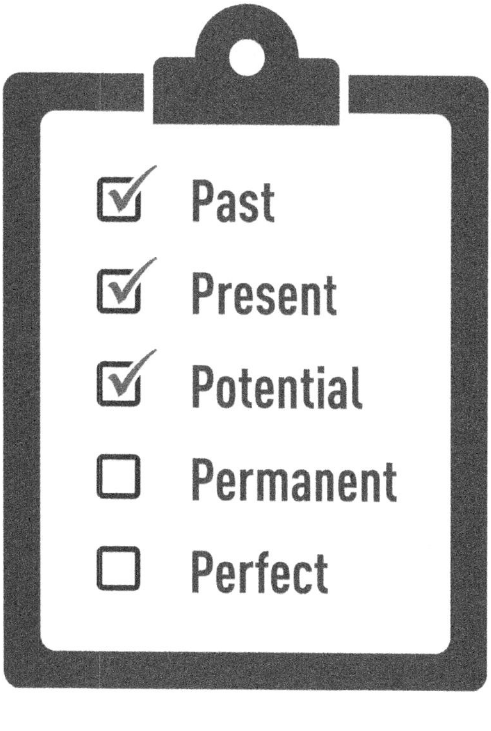

Envision Your Potential

Almost everyone counted Glenn Cunningham out—and he was only seven. Caught in a school fire that severely burned his lower body and killed his older brother, the damage to Glenn's legs and feet was grave; amputation was a strong possibility–if the boy survived infection. When, against all odds, Glenn lived, doctors decreed he would never walk again and brought in a wheelchair.

But Glenn believed he could do better. Much better. With steadfast faith in the power of God, Glenn believed that he had the potential to run—and run fast.

Glenn's belief in his Potential Score was the beginning of a life forged by courage, strength of character, and determination. It was Hebrews 12:1-3 with legs! I love the way *The Message* paraphrases those verses:

> *Do you see what this means—all these pioneers who blazed the way, all these veterans cheering us on? It means we'd better get on with it. Strip down, start running—and never quit! No extra spiritual fat, no parasitic sins. Keep your eyes on Jesus, who both began and finished this race we're in. Study how he did it. Because he never lost sight of where he was headed—that exhilarating finish in and with God—he could put up with anything along the way: Cross, shame, whatever. And now he's there, in the place of honor, right alongside God. When you find yourselves flagging in your faith, go over that story again, item by item, that long litany of hostility he plowed through. That will shoot adrenaline into your souls!* (Hebrews 12:1-3)

Glenn's faith and his commitment to reaching his potential enabled him to overcome insane obstacles.

"I had lost all the flesh on my knees and shins, as well as all the toes on my left foot. My transverse arch was mostly gone,"[13] he recalled.

But that didn't stop him. Glenn's favorite Scripture, Isaiah 40:31, became his encouragement, providing energy and balance:

> *"But those who trust in the Lord will renew their strength; they will soar on wings like eagles, they will run and not grow weary, they will walk and not faint."*(Isaiah 40:31)[14]

Throughout years of hard work and dedication, Glenn began to put one imperfect foot in front of the other. With eyes locked on his potential, he began to run wherever he went. Each month he ran a little farther, a little faster.

And in 1934, **the child doctors said would never walk again became the man who ran the fastest mile in history.** Two years later, Glenn, known as the Iron Horse of Kansas, became the silver medalist in the 1500 meter race at the 1936 Olympics, becoming one of the most legendary distance runners of the 20th century.[15]

Glenn Cunningham's life is a testament to perseverance against incredible odds. It is a testament not to let the past define the future. Glenn's life is a trophy case of pushing past pain, taking control of your present, and doing the hard work required to reach your Potential Score. Glenn went the distance because he shunned excuses and believed in his God-given potential to live his best life. And that made him a champion.

In his book, *The Amazing Power of Positive Thinking*, Norman Vincent Peale wrote, "Glenn Cunningham told me that faith and positive thinking are 85 percent of an athlete's success; in other words, *believing that you can do it*. 'You have to perform on three levels,' Glenn explained, 'physical, mental, and spiritual. And the spiritual helps you draw on power from the Master to help pull you through. And,' he added, 'I don't believe there is such a thing as impossibility.' "[16]

Swing, Batter, Swing

It was 38 years ago, but I'll never forget that baseball field on a beautiful Saturday evening in Haleyville, Alabama. We were playing county baseball. To make the team was an honor. I was the youngest player and had not stood at the plate that week, but I was thrilled to be on the team.

It was the bottom of the ninth, bases loaded and two outs. I heard someone say, "Eads, Coach Rhudy wants you to bat." I remember thinking, *Sure, that's funny*! But it was no joke. I heard Coach yell, "Eads, get your bat!"

Try to picture that moment with me:

- The stands were packed.
- Bases loaded.
- Two outs and the winning team would place first in the tournament.

No pressure at all. I still remember the score 38 years later: *we lost by one*.

Now, that might sound like a counterproductive story to tell in a chapter about potential. There was no movie-script home run for me that day. It was a swing and a miss on the final pitch.

But here's the deal: Coach Rhudy wanted me in the game. So I stepped up to the plate, looked at that field, and took my swings. Even though I didn't get a hit that day, Coach Rhudy's belief in me developed a heart muscle for better swings in the future. He taught me to believe in what could be in the games ahead. He showed me the wisdom of taking my swings.

Wayne Gretzky put potential this way, "You miss 100 percent of the shots you don't take." That's a solid truth in sports and life. **You've got to take shots to reach your potential.**

Sadly, many men and fathers don't see what could be, so they never step up to the plate, never take a swing, never risk a shot, never break into a run. But our children need us to lead them toward the future, show them how to swing for their potential, and run toward a goal.

Propelling Past Resistance

When I begin each day, I like to view every second as a part of my Potential Score—with the understanding that there is no limitation to what I can do for myself and my children through Jesus Christ. I choose to see that potential and believe in it with my heart, soul, mind, and strength.

Will there be misses? Absolutely. Disappointments? Tons of them. But those misses and disappointments can transform us as fathers. They lock our souls on our potential—so we can one day hit the ball out of the park.

Now, before you get too pumped, huddle up and face the reality of pushing to achieve your Potential Score: *There will be obstacles—big ones.* Like a 300-pound, adrenaline-fueled NFL defensive tackle, **Satan makes strategic moves each day to impede you from becoming the man and father you could be. He's mean, nasty, talks a lot of smack, and plays dirty.**

You're going to take some hard hits on the way to reaching your potential as a man and father. There will be days when you bleed. But remember, God has your back—and the vision and strength to catapult you forward. It's His power that can propel you past Satan and toward your potential. When you lean into it, God will make you a winner.

Your Potential Score isn't designated by just one thing; it can be many. I've always wanted to write a book. But year after year, fear and disbelief blocked me like two muddy NFL linebackers.

My cancer diagnosis was like a shot of adrenaline that helped me believe in myself and God's promise that I could do all things through Him. Even though there were days when chemo threatened to beat me to a pulp, I hurled my fear and disbelief to the ground and leaned hard into my potential to write this book. It was a great feeling—like I had pushed right past the impenetrable Ray Lewis! The book you hold in your hands is living proof that we dads can do all things through God, who gives us strength—even when a guy has a chemo drip hooked to his arm.

That's right, achieving your Potential Score one day at a time requires faith in the power of God and belief in yourself, along with the big-muscle push of rigorous determination and discipline. You must believe in your God-given Potential Score and go for it day after day.

One of the main reasons I wrote this book was to model for my sons how to push past obstacles and self-start toward the future. Finishing is tremendous, but starting is essential. The key to effective starting is knowing who you are and what you could be.

So, *who are you? What's your true potential?* Set your sights on that potential because believing is seeing.

Don't Beat Yourself

Many men never start moving toward their potential because they have limited self-worth. Purpose, found in a relationship with Jesus Christ, must bolster self-motivation and self-starting. He gave His life to give us worth! When self-confidence is rooted in God, resilience develops.

> *"Though an army deploys against me, my heart is not afraid;*
> *though a war breaks out against me, still I am confident.*
> *"(Psalm 27:3)*

Jesus created us, and He instructs us to live abundantly in Him. No one can live a truly vibrant and purposeful life without Jesus. He never said life would be easy; He never promised life wouldn't include strikeouts and losses. But Jesus did promise over and over that He would never leave us. He's in the game.

Joshua 1:9 is a pep talk for all men:

> "*Haven't I commanded you: be strong and courageous?* Do *not be afraid or discouraged, for the* Lord *your* God *is with you wherever you go.*" (*Joshua* 1:9)

Isaiah 41:10 serves as a strong arm when energy fades:

> "Do *not fear, for I am with you; do not be afraid, for I am your* God. *I will strengthen you; I will help you; I will hold on to you with My righteous right hand.*" (*Isaiah* 41:10)

And 2 Timothy 1:7 is a slap-on-the-helmet reminder that with God, discipline conquers weakness:

> "For God *has not given us a spirit of fearfulness, but one of power, love, and sound judgment.*" (2 *Timothy* 1:7)

This combination of faith, confidence, and discipline builds the powerful muscle needed to defeat any harmful mind games that impede your Potential Score. Glenn Cunningham once said:

> "*In running, it is man against himself—the cruelest of opponents. The other runners are not the real enemies. The adversary lies within him, in his ability with his brain and heart to master himself and his emotions.*"[17]

Please don't beat yourself, my friend. Don't allow your past to define your future. **Make your life a trophy case of pushing past pain, taking control of your present, and doing the hard work required to reach your Potential Score.** Glenn Cunningham went the distance because he shunned excuses, believed in his potential to live his best life, and ran toward it. He drew upon the power of the Master to pull him through the tough days.

That made him a champion. And you can become a champion too.

Do you see your potential? Do you believe in working hard to live your best life for God's glory? Are you committed to reaching for that potential as a role model for your children? Are you ready to shun excuses and lock your heart, soul, mind, and strength on that potential? Swing, batter, swing!

Believe in Your Child's Potential

When I traveled for work, I often stayed in the West Palm Beach Marriott. The Florida Marlins used the hotel for players who come into their programs in South Florida. I had many opportunities to speak at length with players. Of course, they were all waiting for "the call" that would move them up to the majors.

On one particular night, the young man I was speaking with received that phone call. After a brief conversation, he looked up with a beaming smile and said, "Guys, I made it!"

I will never forget the visual impact of that young man being chosen for the big league. Just moments before the call, we were talking about God. After he finished the call and others congratulated him, he looked back at me and asked, "Shannon, you want to come to the game tomorrow?"

I shook my head and told him I would be watching my son play a Little League game. He smiled, understanding that I would score big for being in the right place. But before that young man walked away, I prayed with him, told him that Jesus loved him, and that he could reach any potential goal with God.

As he walked away, I looked around and spotted flickers of disappointment in a few faces, flickers that asked, *When will I get the call? Why didn't I get picked?* I think a lot of men know that feeling.

My son, Tyler, tried out for middle school basketball; he didn't make the team. The coach told him he wasn't ready and recommended he practice hard and try out again the following year. I believe the coach made the right choice at that season of Tyler's basketball career, but it was a long ride home. Tyler was devastated.

However, my son didn't quit. He came home that day and pounded the hoop in our driveway for hours. Then he practiced every day, and I mean *every day*, for the following year. Not making the team was what Tyler needed to take himself to the next level. It created an inextinguishable fire in him. I remember watching Tyler shoot for hours during a downpour and thinking, *He wants this bad.*

Tyler made the team the next two years in middle school and high school by overcoming his Past Score and working diligently in his present while shooting for his Potential Score.

Colin Powell once said, "A dream doesn't become reality through magic; it takes sweat, determination, and hard work." Tyler didn't believe in magic; he believed in God, himself, and the power of sweat. Sinking shots in the pouring rain taught him a lot about what it took to reach his potential and become a winner. Reaching your potential takes a lot of practice, too—and a lot of time in the rain.

My youngest son, Jase, plays Upward Sports basketball, which teaches young kids godly traits that build self-esteem and confidence through personal accomplishments. Although there's no formal scorekeeping, I remember the first time I told Jase, "Take every opportunity to shoot the ball."

"Why, Dad?" he asked.

I replied, "Because I believe in your potential, son. Practice builds accuracy. You have the potential to score, so believe in yourself and shoot the ball."

So Jase keeps shooting for the basket, aspiring to score, and I continue to celebrate his effort. That's the role of a father—coach, encourager, and visionary of the Potential Score.

After her 2021 Olympic Gold Medal victory in wrestling, Tamyra Mensah-Stock was asked, "When did you first think this was a possibility, that you could be an Olympic Champion?"

Tamyra replied without hesitation, "When I first began wrestling in the tenth grade. I felt I was a natural; it was just about the means of getting there."[18]

But it was the team behind Tamyra, especially her family, that helped propel her toward gold, Tamyra added.

"They were constantly telling me, 'Tamyra, believe in yourself; you've got it. Just go out there and do you, Tamyra. Go out there and get it. The magnitude of that support was what helped me accelerate as quickly as I did."

Tamyra's father died in a car accident on the way home from one of her high school competitions. When asked how she thought her father would have responded to her Olympic win, Tamyra replied in tears, "He would be so proud and would have been the loudest one here. His support is what got me here."

But Tamyra credited God for the real wins in her life.

"In my wildest of dreams I knew I could be an Olympic champion. I prayed I could do it. It was a lot of hard work. I did surprise myself, but it is only by the grace of God that I can even move my feet, so I just leave it in His hands."[19]

Remember, your children are watching you, learning from you. Envision your potential and believe in it because God does. Envision the potential of your children and believe in it because God does. Like Glenn Cunningham and Tamyra Mensah Stock, you and the children you love can accomplish great things when you run toward your potential—and let the Master pull you through.

The Dad Huddle

Guys, if you're looking for a perfect day or time to engage with your children, then you'll never start. If you're looking for a perfect reason, look into your children's eyes. There you'll see that they need you to be at your best. That eye-to-eye contact should instill in you the urgency to begin right now. Delaying the launch to engage fatherhood is a long-term mistake. Begin today!

Scorecard—Your Potential Score Self-assessment

1. Do any old mind scripts play on a loop in your head, talking you out of pursuing your potential?

    •

    •

What steps can you take to replace them with positive affirmations?

    •

    •

2 . Glenn Cunningham became an Olympic champion without toes on his left foot and despite scar tissue restricting his kneecaps. What excuses for not pursuing your potential do you need to leave in the dust behind you?

    •

    •

3. God wires each person to pursue a dream and gifts them to launch it. What dream do you want to resurrect to create a target for your potential?

4. Score yourself in the following areas:

    Prayer: How earnestly are you praying about achieving your Potential Score?

1 2 3 4 5 6 7 8 9 10

Purpose: How grounded in God is your purpose for attaining your Potential Score?

1 2 3 4 5 6 7 8 9 10

Plan: What's your game plan for pursuing your potential?

Where will you start?

What are your success markers?

What designates your finish line?

Pay: Explain how you will generate money to fund the pursuit of your Potential Score.

#4

YOUR PERMANENT SCORE: AFFIRM IT

Your final whistle will blow.

The Crucial End-game

Sports analyst and former NFL head coach Tony Dungy, the father of ten, headlined the 19th annual Athletes in Action Super Bowl breakfast in February 2006. It was his first speaking engagement after the December 2005 funeral for his son, James. At that event, an emotional Dungy said he had learned a lot from his children, "but the most important thing came from James, who would have been 19."[20]

Following is an excerpt from a *Baptist Press* article written by Art Stricklin, who attended the Athletes in Action breakfast.

> *"[James] was a Christian and is today in heaven," Dungy said. He was struggling with the things of the world and took his own life. People ask how I could come back to work so soon. I'm not totally recovered; I don't know if I ever will be, it's still ever-painful," he said, wiping back a tear. "But some good things have come out of it."*
>
> *He said he has received dozens of letters from people who heard him speak at his son's funeral or at a Colts news conference on the peace and assurance he has in his son's salvation and eternal destination. Dungy told of two people having received the gift of sight from his son's donated corneas and of the youth to whom he has talked who are wrestling with similar problems as his son.*
>
> *But Dungy used the most important lesson to drive home his point before the packed ballroom full of former NFL players and coaches, league officials and fans.*
>
> *"If God had talked to me before James' death and said his death would have helped all these people, it would have saved them and healed their sins, but I would have to take your son, I would have said no, I can't do that.*

"But God had the same choice 2,000 years ago with His Son, Jesus Christ, and it paved the way for you and me to have eternal life. That's the benefit I got, that's the benefit James got, and that's the benefit you can get if you accept Jesus into your heart today as your Savior."

Dungy said the biggest regret in his life is that when he saw his son for the last time during the Thanksgiving holidays, he did not hug him when he left but only gave him a casual goodbye.

He said he didn't want to have the same regret at the sold-out breakfast, as he led the crowd in prayer, asking those who did not have Jesus in their life to accept Him for the very first time.

"I want you to know there is a peace in your mind through God's spirit when you know Jesus and know you will be in heaven with Him."[21]

Will your first glimpse of Jesus follow your final glimpse of life on Earth? Your answer to that question determines your Permanent Score, the most important score of all. As humans, we don't do well with endings. But life on this turf called Earth does end. Are you ready for your final whistle?

You tally your Past, Present, and Potential Scores on Earth. Your Permanent Score is settled on Earth but will be eternally celebrated in Heaven with Jesus—or despaired in desolate defeat with never-ending separation from God. The choice is yours.

The Vital Link of the Gospel

Dabo Swinney, head coach of the Clemson Tigers, lives the belief that the Permanent Score is the most important of all because it determines one's place for all eternity. The coach once told the mother of D.J. Uiagalelei, the No. 1 QB recruit of the 2020 class,

"We're going to win some games and lose some games. But I guarantee you that every single player who comes through this program will hear about the gospel of Christ."[22]

You see, the gospel is the vital link to a positive Permanent Score. The gospel is also Dabo's anchor—and he tells his players, "You better have an anchor in life. Bad things happen. If you're not anchored, you're going to be washed away."[23]

The gospel of Christ is both astonishing and straightforward:

☐ **Admit that you're a sinner,** and that no matter how hard you push to reach heaven on your own, it's not doable.

"For all have sinned and fall short of the glory of God." (Romans 3:23)

☐ **Realize that your sin deserves an eternal penalty**—but God made a way out for you.
"For the wages of sin is death, but the gift of God is eternal life in Christ Jesus our Lord." (Romans 6:23)

"For you are saved by grace through faith, and this is not from yourselves; it is God's gift—not from works, so that no one can boast. (Ephesians 2:8-9)

☐ **Believe that Christ died on the cross of Calvary** to pay for your sins so you wouldn't have to, and He rose from the dead three days later to demonstrate His victory over death.

For while we were still helpless, at the appointed moment, Christ died for the ungodly. For rarely will someone die for a just person—though for a good person perhaps someone might even dare to die. But God proves His own love for us in that while we were still sinners, Christ died for us! (Romans 5:6-8)

"For I passed on to you as most important what I also received: that Christ died for our sins according to the Scriptures, that He was buried, that He was raised on the third day according to the Scriptures." (1 Corinthians 15:3-4)

☐ **Embrace Jesus Christ as your personal Savior**. A Permanent Score in heaven is a life-gift purchased by the blood of Jesus and offered freely to those who call upon Him by faith.

"For God loved the world in this way: He gave His One and Only Son, so that everyone who believes in Him will not perish but have eternal life." (John 3:16)

"For everyone who calls on the name of the Lord will be saved." (Romans 10:13)

"For Me, living is Christ and dying is gain." (Philippians 1:21)

☐ **Say a simple, heartfelt prayer,** similar to the following, to affirm your Permanent Score in heaven after your final whistle blows on Earth.

"Dear Lord Jesus, I know that I'm a sinner and that I need You. I believe You died on the cross for me. Please forgive me of my sins. Right now, I turn from them and give my heart and life to You. I receive You as my Savior. Please come into my life and ensure my Permanent Score in heaven with You. Thank You for what You did on the cross for me. Amen."

Faith that Goes the Distance

Dabo's faith has gone the distance throughout the years: pushing past a rough childhood as the son of an alcoholic father. Dabo needed lots of sweat to make the University of Alabama football team as a walk-on wide receiver in 1989 and an unwavering belief in his potential as a coach and a man of God.

"Listen, I come from the most screwed-up dysfunctional situation. You've got violence—police at your house. Your dad's gone. Nowhere to live. I want people to know, if I can make it, anybody can make it," Dabo said.[24]

But to Dabo, "making it" isn't really about game trophies, accolades, or a multi-million-dollar salary. It's about the endgame—when Dabo leaves behind Earth turf and stands before God.

> *"People who know me know that I'm not perfect, but I do try to live my life in a way that hopefully can be pleasing to my Maker because I know that I am going to meet Him one day, and He's not going to pat me on the back and talk to me about how many wins I had, how many coach of the year trophies we got, or how much money I made. I really think he is going to hold me accountable for how I took advantage of the blessings and opportunities that He gave me. The impact that I had on young people. The type of men that we develop through a game."*[25]

Those are the words of a man with a father's heart. Those are the words of a man who knows the Permanent score is the most important of all. Those are the words of a father worth following.

In response to a question about his faith during the 2018 ACC pre-game press conference, Dabo replied:

> *"For me, God and my relationship with Christ have given me hope and peace. I love Jeremiah 29:11, 'For I know the plans I have for you... .' That has been a life verse for me.*

> *[The verse goes on to say], 'to give you hope and a future, plans for good, not disaster.' I've always taken that and applied it to my life along my journey.*
>
> *Everyone sees me now as the head coach of Clemson, but my life has not always been this way. To me, if there is really hope in the future, then there is power in the present to deal with whatever mess you are dealing with in your life. To step through, to hang in there. To preserve and continue to believe in something.*
>
> *That's what my relationship with Christ did for me. It gave me the ability to have hope and belief beyond my circumstances. Dabo went on to say, "The greatest accomplishment that I have had is to see my three sons come to know Christ."*[26]

As fathers, knowing our children have embraced Christ and settled their Permanent Scores is indeed the most significant accomplishment we can achieve. All other scores in life pale in comparison to the Permanent Score. And the choice you make, along with the example you set, heavily weighs the Permanent Score choices your children make.

Where are you leading your children? As men of God and fathers, we must stand firm in our faith to draw our children to God. We must be fathers worth following. Godly leadership is the secret to winning the Fatherhood Game.

Would you please post the following verses where you will face them every day? Commit them to memory to serve as solid-body armor for your mind and spirit.

> *"Just one thing: Live your life in a manner worthy of the gospel of Christ. Then, whether I come and see you or am absent, I will hear about you that you are standing firm in one spirit, with one mind, working side by side for the faith that comes from the gospel."* (Philippians 1:27)

"Therefore, my dear brothers, be steadfast, immovable, always excelling in the Lord's work, knowing that your labor in the Lord is not in vain." (1 Corinthians 15:58)

"Be alert, stand firm in the faith, act like a man, be strong." (1 Corinthians 16:13)

Rod Marinelli, who coached for six seasons with Tony Dungy in Tampa, once said of Dungy's faith, "He never wavers. His faith is unshakeable. Men look for that. I crave it; you're drawn to it as a man."[27]

Are you a father worth following? Is your faith unshakable? Are your children drawn to your faith?

Priceless Peace

Patrick Steben became a deputy sheriff when he was 22. With his training and youthful vigor, he felt bullet-proof. But as time went on, Patrick felt far from bulletproof. He became a father of two daughters, so coming home took on a deeper meaning. Then, two deputies who worked for him died in the line of duty after Patrick was promoted and put in charge of a squad of twelve men.

"I began to feel more and more vulnerable and eventually started abusing prescription medication," Patrick confessed. "When the Sheriff's Office discovered this, I was forced to retire."

Patrick's friends held an intervention, and he entered rehab.

"It was the lowest point in my life," he admitted. "When I left rehab, I thought about suicide numerous times. The only thing that kept me from doing it was my two daughters.

"I felt lost, alone, and scared," Patrick admitted. Then Pastor Eads asked me to walk with him one night. We didn't talk about God or Jesus or salvation; we were just two men walking and talking sports.

"But I kept walking with him day after day, and we started talking about Jesus. He explained how Jesus died on the cross for me and my sins. I asked a lot of questions. He gave me a Bible and invited me to church. I was terrified walking into that church for the first time, but I started attending regularly.

"On Easter Sunday, I accepted Christ in front of the church and my family. I gained a lot of peace that day, knowing that I was going to heaven when my time on Earth was up."

Patrick had settled his Permanent Score, but he wanted more. He wanted to know that his wife and daughters would join him in heaven. And he wanted to lead them there.

"One afternoon, we all sat down in our dining room with Pastor Eads. He and I explained to them why people put their faith in Jesus. They all accepted Christ right there in our home. It was such a relief," Patrick recalls. "The peace I have knowing we will spend the rest of eternity together is priceless."

A priceless peace. **As a father, I have no greater hunger for peace than knowing that my sons, Tyler and Jase, will spend eternity in heaven with me and my wife, Michelle.**

Recently Tyler shared the following words with a friend of mine, and to say they made this father's heart glad would be the understatement of the year.

> *The grace of God alone established my permanent score, but my Dad led the way. As far back as second grade, I can remember the example he set by teaching me to trust and obey Jesus Christ as Lord and Savior.*
>
> *Dad's example is humble and heroic. It's humble because he surrenders himself to Jesus every moment of every day. His example is heroic because God uses him in amazing ways to further the kingdom of our Lord Jesus Christ.*
>
> *My dad's example led me to confidence in the sacrifice of Jesus on the cross. It wasn't that Dad has divine power or authority but that he has faith in Jesus Christ, who holds all power and authority.*

> *I thank God every day that my dad is in my life because not only does he bring me confirmation that I'm a child of God, he brings me the conviction I need to leave this world behind and follow Jesus Christ to heaven.*

Game Over

Let me be transparent; I have stage three cancer. Although that diagnosis involves brutal days I'd rather skip, I'm still quite attached to Earth turf. I'm not ready to lace up my cleats for the last time. But when God says, "Eads, you're up!" I'm prepared to step into eternity. Because I've settled my Permanent Score, I'm filled with hope as I move around on both smooth and rough Earth turf.

In an "All Pro Dads" blog, Tony Dungy summed up the release of hope for the future:

> *"... as Christians we do have hope for the future. This life isn't everything. We have and can hold onto the promises of God that there is going to be a life for us that is going to be everlasting, beautiful, filled with joy, and devoid of pain. When I think about that future, that's what keeps me going. When I face the ups and downs in life, problems and troubles, and little setbacks I think about going forward to a place where I'm not going to have to worry about any of that.*
> *No matter what has happened to me on earth, it's going to be a time of great celebration and joy. It gives me hope, and it's what I think about when I think of heaven."*[28]

In John 3:16, God gives us a life-altering promise—and a choice: "For God loved the world in this way: He gave His one and only Son, so that everyone who believes in Him will not perish but have eternal life."

Your eternal destination depends on the choice you make about your Permanent Score. When you choose Jesus, you can walk through good and bad days on Earth filled with unwavering hope for the future. It's a beautiful Permanent Score filled priceless peace.

The Dad Huddle

Dads, we need to lead our families to the final whistle with confidence. Our children need us to focus on God's plan. One way to improve this focus is to study God's Word. When I'm out of the Word of God, I'm not focused

A second way is to pray. I'm aligned when I spend time in prayer with God daily.

A third way is to keep all lines of communication open with your children. Use words carefully. Be careful not to destroy what takes years to rebuild.

The final whistle is coming, and when you hear that sound, your Fatherhood Game is over. Prepare well for the final whistle. It's vital for you and your children.

Scorecard—Your Permanent Score Self-assessment

1. Do you know Jesus Christ as your personal Lord and Savior? Yes or No

   If *yes*, tell someone your salvation story or write it here.

   If not, what is preventing you from changing your Permanent Score while you have the opportunity?

   If you have questions and would like to speak with someone about this important decision, ask the person who gave you your copy of *Winning the Fatherhood Game* or contact the church sponsoring the fatherhood event.

2. What are you doing to guide the Permanent Scores of your children?

3. Are you doing anything that may be driving your children away from a Permanent Score in heaven with God?

#5

YOUR PERFECT SCORE: ACHIEVE IT

But you'll have to wait.

The Thrill of Victory & the Agony of Defeat

On February 2, 1997, Jeremy Sonnenfeld bowled three perfect games, achieving the first 900 series certified by the American Bowling Congress. *Three perfect games.* I cannot imagine bowling one 300-game; I would be thrilled with a 200!

Nadia Comaneci and Mary Lou Retton. What do these spectacular gymnasts have in common? They both won gold medals for achieving perfect tens in the Olympics, Nadia on uneven bars and Mary Lou on vault.

Since Major League Baseball's inception in 1876, there have been 313 no-hitters. According to the official MLB website, "Throwing a no-hitter is a pretty uncommon feat on its own, and throwing more than one is even rarer. Thirty-five pitchers have thrown at least two no-hitters."[29]

Nolan Ryan stands at the top of the list, throwing *seven* no-hitters and striking out almost 6,000 batters. **Throughout his long career, Nolan Ryan's arm exhibited the muscle and motion of perfection.**

These athletes have proved that perfection in sports is doable. However, living a perfect life is not. In that arena, everyone loses because there's no chance for victory, just the agony of defeat! Scripture makes this reality clear:

> *"There is certainly no righteous man on the earth who does good and never sins."* (Ecclesiastes 7:20)
>
> *"For all have sinned and fall short of the glory of God."* (Romans 3:23)

Only Jesus Christ, the Son of God, mastered perfection during his years on Earth. And while none of us can achieve that goal, Jesus puts the desire for it in the hearts of those who believe in Him, so we'll never settle for less.

I like the way *The Message* paraphrases 2 Corinthians 5:1-5 because it's so visual:

"*For instance, we know that when these bodies of ours are taken down like tents and folded away, they will be replaced by resurrection bodies in heaven—God-made, not handmade—and we'll never have to relocate our "tents" again. Sometimes we can hardly wait to move—and so we cry out in frustration. Compared to what's coming, living conditions around here seem like a stopover in an unfurnished shack, and we're tired of it! We've been given a glimpse of the real thing, our true home, our resurrection bodies! The Spirit of God whets our appetite by giving us a taste of what's ahead. He puts a little of heaven in our hearts so that we'll never settle for less.*" (*2 Corinthians* 5:1-5)

The "heaven in our hearts" propels us to strive for godly lives on Earth, not just for ourselves as Christ-followers but for those watching our lives, especially our children. Hebrews 12:1 tells us:

> "*Therefore, since we also have such a large cloud of witnesses surrounding us, let us lay aside every weight and the sin that so easily ensnares us. Let us run with endurance the race that lies before us.*" (*Hebrews* 12:1)

As a believer in Jesus Christ, I don't need to achieve perfection on Earth because Jesus is and will always be my Perfect Score. Yours too. However, don't think for a moment that we can be lazy in our walks with Christ. His perfection empowers us to lean in and move in that direction. Vince Lombardi understood the benefit of chasing perfection:

> "*Perfection is not attainable, but if we chase perfection, we can catch excellence.*" – Vince Lombardi [30]

The Apostle Paul put it this way, with athletic prowess I might add:

> *"Run in such a way to win the prize. Now everyone who competes exercises self-control in everything. However, they do it to receive a crown that will fade away, but we a crown that will never fade away. Therefore I do not run like one who runs aimlessly or box like one beating the air. Instead, I discipline my body and bring it under strict control, so that after preaching to others, I myself will not be disqualified."* (1 Corinthains 9:24b-27)

As long-distance runners in the race of life, God commands us to be like Jesus. In 2 Corinthians 5:17, we are told:

> *"Therefore, if anyone is in Christ, he is a new creation; old things have passed away, and look, new things have come."* (2 Corinthians 5:17)

I want to be clear; we cannot achieve perfection on this third rock from the sun. But through the power of the Holy Spirit, we place our imperfect lives in His perfect hands. We embrace the perfection of Jesus, surrender to His ways, and commit to following Him wherever, whenever, and however.

> *So here's what I want you to do, God helping you: Take your everyday, ordinary life—your sleeping, eating, going-to-work, and walking-around life—and place it before God as an offering. Embracing what God does for you is the best thing you can do for him. Don't become so well-adjusted to your culture that you fit into it without even thinking. Instead, fix your attention on God. You'll be changed from the inside out. Readily recognize what he wants from you, and quickly respond to it. Unlike the culture around you, always dragging you down to its level of immaturity, God brings the best out of you, develops well-formed maturity in you."*
> (Romans 12:1-2 The Message)

Eye on the Prize

The best part of living for Jesus is that one day you will be perfect. *What? Hold on, Shannon, you said achieving a Perfect Score is impossible.*

That's correct; you'll never achieve a Perfect Score on Earth. But you will have a Perfect Score in heaven!

You see, **life on Earth is not a sprint of perfection but a marathon toward perfection in heaven with Jesus.** We're humans who make mistakes on Earth, but in heaven, we'll be perfect like Jesus *because of what Jesus did for us on Earth*. Our bodies, minds, and spirits will one day be perfect. That's mind-boggling—and amazing!

I feel woefully inadequate in describing how perfect heaven will be; however, it's the dwelling place of God. That means no one can abide there who isn't perfect.

In heaven, human imperfections are gone. Everyone there will be perfect in Jesus. We won't be equal to Jesus, nor will we be deities, but we will be new in His glory. Our old ways, bodies, and imperfections? History. Our earthbound problems and imperfections? Eliminated. Amen to that! No wrinkles, no torn ACLs, no need for Aleve or Relief Factor!

As you put mile after mile on your running shoes during your trek on Earth, remember, perfection is achievable—but you'll have to wait for it. When you settle your Permanent Score on Earth with faith in Jesus Christ, your Perfect Score awaits you in heaven. Your entry there will be the perfect beginning in eternity for an imperfect life lived on Earth.

The Dad Huddle:

Dads, we need one another. We need dad-to-dad accountability to finish the Fatherhood Game as winners. When we're at our best, we should be helping other fathers up. When we're down, we should humbly reach for the extending hands of other dads. We're in this game together, and fathers striving to be more like Jesus can impact the world in a big way. So, let's get after it together.

Scorecard—Your Perfect Score Self-assessment

1. How prone are you to demand perfection of yourself and others?

   1 2 3 4 5 6 7 8 9 10

2. What are you doing to replace false urges for worldly satisfaction with actions that reflect Jesus?

   -
   -
   -

3. What area(s) of your life do you need to give to God to bring out the best in yourself for His glory?

   -
   -
   -

4. List two steps you can take this week to realign your focus from perfectionism to being your best on Earth as a follower of Christ, knowing that perfection is yet to come in heaven.

   -

   -

5. How are you sharing with your kids the dangers of perfectionism and the importance of heaven's Perfect Score?

SECTION 3
BUILDING YOUR MENTOR MUSCLE

Man-to-Man Mentoring

In 1997 Ken Carter could have coached student-athletes at several elite high schools in California. Instead, he chose the banged-up basketball court of Richmond High, embedded in a drug-invested, gang-saturated area of the state.

Why did Coach Carter choose that banged-up court? Because he had the heart of a mentor and saw those Richmond athletes not just as players but young men who needed a mentor. He cared enough to step out of his comfort zone and into a hard-court challenge—where he faced pushback from both players and parents. That mentoring role wasn't easy; it took time, effort, patience, and persistence. But the results were herculean.

One of Coach Carter's most pivotal moments came in 1999 when he benched his unbeaten team for poor academics. Every player under his influence graduated; some went on to attend college. Because of Carter's accountability stance, those young men not only upped their grades, they learned how to play smart in sports—and life.

Man-to-man mentoring changes lives. If you've seen the movie *Coach Carter*, you realize that he showed those young men how to use the light of God within them to help each other. When one player was down, the others stepped up physically to help him complete required pushups and suicide drills. More importantly, those young men stepped up mentally, emotionally, and spiritually. They became strong men. That's the momentum of mentoring.

At one point in the movie, the player who had initially given Coach Carter the most resistance stands and quotes a poem, thanking him for saving their lives:

> *"Our deepest fear is not that we are inadequate. Our deepest fear is that we are powerful beyond measure. It is our light, not our darkness, that most frightens us. ...We are*

> *all meant to shine, as children do. We were born to make manifest the glory of God that is within us. ... And as we let our own light shine, we unconsciously give other people permission to do the same. As we are liberated from our own fear, our presence automatically liberates others."*[31]

As men of God, we can liberate other men from fear through mentoring. We can shine the mighty glory of God that is within us—and give other men permission to do the same. Just as Coach Carter's tenure at Richmond High School is an example of the light of Philippians 4:9 with legs, our time on Earth can manifest light slam-dunked with the liberating legs of mentoring.

> "Do *what you have learned and received and heard and seen in me, and the God of peace will be with you."* (*Philippians* 4:9)

Ordinary Men in Action

When Jesus began his ministry, He chose twelve ordinary men to mentor, giving us a vivid picture of the process of mentoring: quality time used to share godly wisdom and lend support.

Men playing the Fatherhood Game desperately need other men to share the wisdom and experience they've already gained in the game. Men also need accountability to keep them on track. And fathers need balance in their lives modeled by others who have learned it through taking some spills of their own.

Man-to-man mentoring is the process of living Matthew 28:19a and Proverbs 13:20 out loud as ordinary men with an extraordinary calling.

> *"Go therefore and make disciples of all nations."* (*Matthew* 28:19*a*)

"The one who walks with the wise will become wise, but a companion of fools will suffer harm." (Proverbs 13:20)

The Smell of Jesus

How does a guy find the right mentor? Well, no one goes to a baseball field looking for a tennis coach. Looking in the right place is the first step in identifying a good mentor.

First, **I believe that a man with solid mentor muscle will have the smell of Jesus on him because he has built that by bulking up with truths of Scripture.** He studies the Bible daily for guidance. He commits Scripture to memory for strength and confidence because God's Word is inspired, inherent, and infallible. Repeated reps of Bible verses don't tire him; they inspire him. And a man with mentor muscle prays long and hard because prayer is his armor.

If a man smells like Jesus, he'll also be in church. Godly mentoring must be grounded in the Bible, and a godly mentor will play an active role in a vibrant Christian church.

God has put the church in our lives to build up the spiritual body. Churches should exist to build up men. They should be in the discipleship business. A godly mentor grows his faith by being a disciple and guiding other men.

Asking for Help

Of course, asking another man for help is tough for most guys. Asking someone to invest in your future can be awkward. *What if he says no?*

But we guys often forget that we ask for help every day. When we order food, we ask for help. When we speak into our phones for directions, we're asking for help. When we search Google, we're asking for help. When we go to any medical office, we're asking for help.

Truth is, when we want something bad enough, we'll ask. And where mentoring is concerned, asking the right guy for his help is crucial. That's why asking Jesus for help when seeking a mentor is the right first move. He always knows what's best for you. He knows your ideal mentor match. So, ask Him to connect you with the right man for the coaching job.

Remember, godly mentors aren't perfect, but they smell like Jesus, look like Jesus, talk like Jesus, and act like Jesus. With your prayer for a mentor guiding you, look around. What men in your circle are in that kind of shape? Who among them has a personality that draws you? Use Hebrews 13:7 as a launchpad toward the mentor who is right for you.

> *"Remember your leaders who have spoken God's word to you. As you carefully observe the outcome of their lives, imitate their faith."* (*Hebrews* 13:7)

Here's a checklist for connecting with a godly mentor.

- ☐ Ask Jesus to help you find your mentor match.
- ☐ Look in the right place to find that person.
- ☐ Ask your church staff for suggestions.
- ☐ Observe how other men communicate the truths of the gospel.
- ☐ Spend time around an individual before you ask him to mentor you.
- ☐ Have the confidence to ask.
- ☐ Commit to the process of being mentored.

Step Up

Now, let's put the athletic shoe on the other foot. Mentors should take a proactive approach instead of a reactive stance. If we as Christian men and fathers continue to wait on guys to ask us to mentor them, we're out of step with the discipleship mandated by the gospel of Jesus Christ.

Seasoned men of the church should be proactively asking God for other men to mentor. God commissions us to do it. He mandates godly men to mentor others. There are men in your arena praying for a mentor, so don't wait around to be asked. Proactively ask God to connect you to a guy you can mentor.

Just as the Apostle Paul mentored Timothy, each of us needs a Timothy in our life. Who is your Timothy? Think about this: *what if every Christian man mentored two men every year*? That compound math would change the world.

> *"Iron sharpens iron, and one man sharpens another."* (Proverbs 27:17)

For the record, I'm advocating a mentoring relationship of need, not neediness. Healthy mentoring means you speak into someone's life, not that you run it. Jesus would never place someone in your life for you to control and dictate their every move. Guys do need the camaraderie of someone who understands their struggles, temptations, and fears because he has battled them too. That means the first step for both a mentor and a mentee is humbleness, followed by laying aside selfish pride.

In the final moments of the movie *Schindler's List*, Oskar Schindler received the gift of gold ring engraved with, "Whoever saves one life saves the world entire." If the church could grasp this compounding concept, manhood and fatherhood would forever change for the better. We men of God would be in shape and focused on our calling:

> *"Know well the condition of your flock, and pay attention to your herds."*(Proverbs 27:23)

Fear is Normal

Most Christian men desire to grow in their faith. However, where mentoring is concerned, fear holds many back—the fear of rejection, the fear of the unknown, and the fear of accountability.

Because fear is a reality in our everyday lives, it's understandable to have fear when mentoring another man or being mentored by someone. But do you think the disciples followed Jesus without fear? No! While it's OK to feel fearful, please don't allow it to control your life. Jesus isn't the author of fear. He leads men with faith, hope, and love.

> *"Do not fear, for I am with you."* (*Isaiah 41:10a*)

On the flip side, Satan is clever, and he plays a lot of mind games to keep guys out of the game. Satan loves to convince men they are unworthy of Jesus. He wants us guys to doubt our self-worth, to drown in our imperfections.

It's a lot harder for Satan to tear a guy down with discouraging words when that guy is building himself up with godly counsel. That's why man-to-man mentoring is so vital. Mentoring is muscle-building weight training for defeating Satan and correcting misguided thinking about achieving perfection on Earth.

Guys, hit the court and seize the momentum of man-to-man mentoring. If you're a Paul, find your Timothy. If you're a Timothy, search for your Paul. (Most likely, he's right there in your local church or small group.)

It's time to man up. It's time to change the world one man at a time. Remember, "Whoever saves one life saves the world entire."

6 Tips for a Mentor

1. **Ask yourself:** *Who can I help? When can I help? How can I help? Where can I help? Why should I help?*
2. **Move slowly.** Slow and easy is the best approach for pouring into someone's life.
3. **Allow your mentee to reveal** where he is in life. Every journey can contain a lot of baggage.
4. **Listen.** Become that safe place where your mentee can get things off his chest without condemnation.
5. **Ask about** his dreams and goals. Time and kindness are the two best medicines for dealing with life.
6. **Imagine the power** of multiplication if everyone helped someone. Who is your Timothy, your one?

7 Tips for the Church

1. **Start** small with a few godly men.
2. **Educate** about the WHY of mentoring.
3. **Make** it an easy process to mentor men.
4. **Train** leaders to make mentoring effective.
5. **Create** an easy onboarding process.

6. **Celebrate** success stories.

7. **Maintain** a clear vision.

Mentoring the Fatherless

Bobby Bowden was one of the winningest coaches in NCAA history. When he first arrived at Florida State in 1976, the Seminole program had won only four games over the previous three seasons. Fans in the stands were sparse.

In *The Bowden Way*, his book on leadership written with his son Steve, the coach stated:

> *"When I was at Alabama the bumper stickers read 'Beat Auburn.' When I was at West Virginia they read 'Beat Pitt.' When I came to F.S.U., the bumper stickers read 'Beat Anybody.'"*[32]

Bowden rewrote that Florida State bumper sticker with gridiron ink. Under his leadership, the Seminoles beat most everybody. His teams finished in the top five of the Associated Press rankings every season from 1987 to 2000. The Seminoles were unbeaten in bowl games from 1982 to 1995 and won national championships in 1993 and 1999.[33]

Bowden's passion for the game moved the football time and time again. However, it was Bowden's unswerving faith as a follower of Jesus that changed the lives of many young men on his teams.

You see, **Bobby Bowden had a heart for the fatherless, and he took it as his calling to stand in the gap.**

"For the fatherless receives compassion in You." (Hosea 14:3b)

In a Christian Broadcasting Network (CBN) article Bowden stated the following about players on his teams:

> *"I believe young men need a male in the home. Young boys raised need a male figure in the home. It's not what most of them got ... somebody to discipline them. . . I take them to*

church, have Bible reading with them, and pray at supper. I think that myself and the staff add a lot."[34]

Bowden gave the fatherless young men on his team discipline. But first, he gave them Jesus.

"It starts with Jesus – He forgave," said Bowden, who called the day he accepted Jesus as his savior his "biggest win." "My mother and my dad, they saw that I learned to read the Bible and how to pray and took me to church. So as a football coach, I told my coaches, 'We gotta be daddy for these boys because a lot of them don't have one.' We might be the closest thing he'll ever know to a daddy and that's the approach we tried to take, and I tried to teach them the same principles I was taught."[35]

Being a daddy for those fatherless boys was a role Bowden believed God gave him, along with football as a witnessing field.

"I don't know of any football player that played for me who didn't know about Jesus. Talk about getting their attention, every Friday night before a football game, they were going to listen to you. I would read Scripture to them. I get letters from (former) players and not one of them mention football. Not one of them. They say, coach, 'Thank You.'"[36]

At Bowden's memorial service in 2021, Jimbo Fisher, former head coach of Florida State and current head coach of Texas A&M, said of his mentor:

"You knew what he stood for with his relationship with God ... He was the epitome of the example of what a coach should be, a mentor, a guy of leadership." [37]

Be Like Bowden

Deuteronomy 10:18 megaphones men of faith to be like Bowden, who stepped onto the field God gave him to be like Jesus.

> *"He executes justice for the fatherless and the widow, and loves the foreigner, giving him food and clothing."* (*Deuteronomy* 10:18)

God calls men of faith to step onto the fields He has given us and into the void where fatherless boys live. They need us to show them Jesus. To listen to them. To teach them about manhood. To share meals. To play ball with them. And to welcome them into the open arms of the church. It's mentoring in all its aspects: spiritual, physical, practical, mental, and emotional.

Mentoring the fatherless is a calling godly men must embrace. **A stunning 23.6 percent of US children (17.4 million) lived in father-absent homes in 2014.**[38] Results from a sample of 835 juvenile male inmates found that father absence was the only disadvantage on the individual level with significant effects on gun carrying, drug trafficking, and co-occurring behavior. Individuals from father-absent homes were 279 percent more likely to carry guns and deal drugs than peers living with their fathers.[39]

Those are horrible statistics men of God can and must change. We're equipped to do it and called to do it. And, like Bobby Bowden learned, mentoring is the math that adds up to changed lives. Mentoring can transform the faltering fatherless into winning men of God. We must take the field because we are needed more than ever.

The crisis before us is urgent. The church must step up and impact the fatherless. Remember that all Christians are adopted. What we forget is that Jesus desires to adopt everyone. Jesus wants every child. We as fathers need to consider what we can do to impact the fatherless in our communities. Time is of the essence. **If every man of faith influenced one fatherless child, together, we could change the world.**

The Forms of Fatherlessness

His name is Jase, and he's terrific. Smart. Handsome. Loves pizza. Reading and math are his favorite subjects. Jase runs fast and wants to be outside all day long. He never meets a stranger. He's an awesome kid.

By God's amazing grace, Jase is my gotcha-son. The story from the social worker is that his biological father refused to step up when told that Jase was his son. He shut his heart on Jase when he shut his front door in the social worker's face.

But Jase's story doesn't stop there. It's where his story begins. He was two days old the first time my wife, Michelle, and I saw him. We fought over who would hold him first. Now, six years later, he's growing fast and happy. Jase brings laughter into our home. I'm thrilled to call him my son. He's no longer fatherless, and our house flows with joy because of him.

Fatherlessness comes in different forms: deceased dads, fathers who come in and out of the picture, fathers who live in the home but never engage in their children's lives, and those who leave to go to another home. There's heartbreak in every scenario.

Safe Places

Jesus must be our foundation when we seek to mentor fatherless children. It's essential to keep them safe. We must constantly remind ourselves about evil and evildoers who want to cause harm. As men of faith, we want to make their lives better, and mentoring them with the good news of Jesus is life-changing.

> *"Provide justice for the needy and the fatherless; uphold the rights of the oppressed and the destitute."* (Psalm 82:3)

Here are some safe places to mentor the fatherless.

After-school programs. Some churches offer after-school mentoring programs for the fatherless. If your church doesn't, consider developing one with the guidance of church staff.

Tutoring. Many kids need help with some form of education. Look for Christian agencies in your area that help kids with homework.

Sports. A vast majority of kids love sports. Programs like Upward Sports, Fellowship of Christian Athletes, and the YMCA have programs where you can volunteer to speak into the lives of the fatherless.

Necessary Self-Protection

Remember this: we live in a different world than most of us grew up in years ago. We must protect the children while protecting ourselves.

Sadly, there will always be people who choose to accuse. Protecting yourself as a mentor to the fatherless is vital. It is wise to select mentoring programs with structure and accountability protocols (YMCA, Upward Sports, First Priority, and Fellowship of Christian Athletes). I cannot emphasize this enough.

Mentoring the fatherless has tremendous ministry potential for the church. **With safeguards for mentors and fatherless children in place, local churches could become the hub for life change.** Here are four things churches can do to develop ministries that mentor fatherless children.

1. Offer educational training within the church.
2. Provide a safe space for mentoring within the church.
3. Work with schools that are close to the church.
4. Develop a strategy to impact neighborhoods near the church.

The Simple Ministry of Playing Ball

One month before I learned I had cancer, God laid a burden on my heart: go with Tyler into a government housing complex in Tampa, minister to children there, many who are fatherless. The calling of John 14:18 guided us.

> "*I will not leave you as orphans; I am coming to you.*"

I knew we needed to start small and be proactive in our approach. We, along with three other fathers and their sons, approached the management team of the housing development near us. They gave us the thumbs up.

I will never forget that first Saturday morning. We took 100 footballs, 100 basketballs, and 100 soccer balls. After we exited our cars, we prayed for wisdom, compassion, guidance, and protection. Then, we began to throw a football. It only took a few minutes before kids started spilling out of their apartments to play a game with us.

Within an hour, the hundreds of balls we brought were in the hands of smiling kids. As we were leaving, a little boy and his sister approached me and said they were not allowed to come out to play until he completed his chores. He asked if there were two basketballs left. I was heartbroken because they were all gone. I prayed, *Lord, please let there be just one basketball somewhere, please.*

About that time, Tyler came around the corner, carrying two basketballs. You should have seen the faces of those two kids light up! Tyler was grinning as much as they were!

Tyler and I were able to do our ball giveaway event one more time before I began chemo treatments. We're both looking forward to when my health numbers are strong enough for us to continue this ministry because we know that something as simple as playing ball with a fatherless child can impact generations to come. That is the power of mentoring the fatherless.

"And what you have heard from me in the presence of many witnesses, commit to faithful men who will be able to teach others also." (2 Timothy 2:2)

SECTION 4

MAKE WINNING PERSONAL

Your Legacy of Wisdom

Because a father's legacy impacts the future, I've included in this section some life-coaching wisdom for my sons, Tyler and Jase. I believe your children and mine need and want this type of coaching. It makes winning the Fatherhood Game personal.

I hope you'll consider compiling a legacy of wisdom for your children that will coach them in the game of life when you're around—and when you're not. You can do this with letters, audio recordings, texts, or whatever format resonates with you. Don't hesitate to use technology to keep you in the game with your children and others you mentor.

Here are some of the texts I've sent my sons. Michelle also prints them out and places them in a folder for safekeeping.

God's Will

Tyler and Jase, lose your life in God's will, and He will save you in His plan and purpose. Keep Matthew 16:25 as your motto: "For whoever wants to save his life will lose it, but whoever loses his life because of Me will find it."

Dream Big

Boys, embrace a dream not easily accomplished. Writing my first book fulfilled one of my dreams! At times, it was like doing full-court suicide drills—lots and lots of sweat and back-and-forth motion but so worth the struggle when I crossed that finish line. Learn to thirst for the thrill of victory and sweat hard to get there.

Thirst for Victory

Boys, learn to thirst for the thrill of victory and sweat hard to get there.

Know Your Data

Tyler and Jase, if there's anything in the past that needs your attention, settle the issue immediately. You'll win some and lose some. It's what you do with the data of winning and losing that will empower you to move beyond the past and into tomorrow.

Live Large

Boys, squeeze every second you can from each day lived. Don't allow anyone or anything to rob you of your scoring ability. It's what you do today that affects your ability to achieve your potential tomorrow.

Develop Your Muscles

Boys, unless I give you a chance to stand on your own, I'll have to carry you for the rest of your life. My back is not that strong, boys, so develop the muscles you need to move forward as men.

Run

Tyler and Jase, used trophies can be bought, but you earn your potential scores. Fix your eyes on Jesus, and He will lead you to success. Your potential is waiting; never stop running toward it.

Avoid Debt

Don't become a slave to debt. Live on a budget. Control your money, or money will control you. Remember, you'll never be generous if you are bound to debt.

Learn Balance

Boys, balance is essential in life. Kids have to be kids, and I want you to be kids, teenagers, and young adults who laugh, jump, run, and have fun. These are essential activities needed to balance your daily responsibilities.

Letters to My Sons

Few people write letters these days. Even fewer write letters to their children. I've written letters to mine because I want them to know, whether I'm with them on Earth or in heaven, I'll always be in their corner. Living with cancer has taught me to seize life by the horns and do everything possible today to prepare my sons for tomorrow.

Here are some of the letters I've written to my sons. I hope you take the time to write to your children, so they'll always know that you're in their corner—loving them, coaching them, and helping them win in life.

Jase and Tyler,
Thank you for being my boys. I'm a blessed man because of you two.

Where do I even begin to tell you how much your mom and I love you? While you two are different in many ways, you're identical in some of your needs. You just want our love and Chick-fil-A every day!

You both amaze me with how smart you are. How much information you soak up. How energetically you move. How thoughtful and kind you are in your different stages of life. Keep that up!

I'm excited to watch you grow up as I coach you through life as men of God. I won't always have perfect advice, but I'll always try to listen.

My cancer challenge taught me how important it is to lose your life in God's will because He will save you in His plan and purpose. I pray that you love Jesus, serve Him, worship Him, listen to Him, and wait on Him. Waiting is hard, but it builds up the inner soul.

Love,
Dad

Tyler and Jase,
Every decision you make has consequences. As you grow up, your mom and I will slowly release decision-making to you as you learn how your choices impact everyday life. We love and raise you equally, discipline you accordingly, and guide you purposefully as we provide for your needs.

When you read through Winning the Fatherhood Game, *think about what you could be and will be in God's timing. Never place my book above the Bible, but I want you to fully grasp the importance of the Five Vital Scores in life. Within those stages is where you will live, learn, love, lose, laugh, lead, look, listen—and even be lazy some days. That's life!*

Know that I'll do everything possible to minimize obstacles that could damage your scores. In the end, however, your choices and score results are yours and yours alone.

As your dad, I want to help you understand the impact of your Past Scores and coach you to develop plans for your Present Scores. I also want to encourage you to believe in your Potential Scores while helping you understand the truth about your Perfect Scores.

Most importantly, I want to lead you to Permanent Scores that embrace eternity in heaven. In life, you'll score and be scored. You'll win some and lose some. It's what you do with the data of winning and losing that will empower you to move beyond the past and into tomorrow.

Love,
Dad

Jase and Tyler,
One of the most important things I've ever given you is my last name. No golden spoon is attached to it, but it does come with respect. Wear the name proudly. I've worked diligently to keep it honorable and expect you to do the same.

There'll be days when you might question my parenting rules, reasoning, and demands. Know that your mom and I take firm stands because we love you. When you become parents, you'll thank us.

Character and honesty are two key attributes I hope to instill in you both, along with a love for Jesus and a strong work ethic. I'm not looking for perfect boys because there is no perfect parent. What I hope is for you to avoid Past Scores that take years to erase.

Love,
Dad

Boys,

One of my jobs as your dad is to show you the world: the good, the bad, and the ugly. That way, you can navigate it with agility. Your mom and I have built everything on Jesus. We offer no apologies or regrets for doing that.

Growing up in a minister's home has put larger bullseyes on your backs, boys. We're raising you with morals, ethics, and conviction—which is difficult when some of your friends live each day with few restrictions. I say "no" a lot because I'm looking out for you today so that you will fill your tomorrows with positive choices.

Unfortunately, there will be people who will not like you or what you stand for. Jesus told us that the world would hate us because we stand for what's right. That's reality.

Don't waste your time trying to please others. Look inward and upward in God's strength and purpose for your life. Seek to please Him.

Most people would pay big bucks for a do-over. Looks, appearances, titles, corner offices, and other attractive things can cloud your judgment about which team you should be on. To stay focused:

1. *Keep your eyes on Jesus.*
2. *Build onward and upward by proactively confronting the bad days in your life and celebrating the good ones.*
3. *Grow from your mistakes, but do not give up.*
4. *Never quit.*

Love,
Dad

Jase and Tyler,
Always start with God. Everything else will be out of alignment until you balance that relationship. Just like a car that's out of alignment, you'll pull to the left or right while never going straight.

After you've confirmed your alignment with God, go to the next step: family. Marriage is an example of choosing and being chosen. Don't settle for a woman you can live with. Search for the one you cannot live without. Yes, there are many potential catches in the ocean, and you'll notice a lot of them along the way. Catch the right one, and she'll love you forever.
Love,
Dad

Boys,
Interruptions are part of life. Timeouts have no pre-ordained check-in time, so don't freak out when they happen. Interruptions won't overtake you unless you allow them. Throughout my timeouts, I've seen God move in amazing ways.

Tyler, I remember when your mom and I spoke with you about my timeouts and what was needed to keep moving forward. You were a trooper, and you continue to fight for me. Jase, when you get a bit older, we'll walk you through interruptions too, but I know you have the strong spirit to face them.

Timeouts allow us to catch our breath, get some water, rest, and receive coaching. Boys, your timeouts in life won't be the same as mine, but sometimes they'll knock the wind out of you, as mine did me. When that happens, catch your breath, exhale prayers to God, and hold on to those you love. Eventually, you'll get back in the game. Be patient and trust God.
Love,
Dad

Boys,

Quitting is easy. People do it every day. If you ever feel like quitting something, call your mom or me. One thing she and I promised each other was to stick together "until death do us part." That's a commitment we'll keep so you boys can witness the beauty and bounty of it.

When looking at a tombstone, you see the birth date and the death date of an individual. But it's the dash between those dates that matters most. Some people choose to quit and stop living years ahead of their death.

You cannot control the starting or ending dates of your life in life, but you can control the dash. That dash is powerful, and it's yours to live. Live your dash well, and never quit!

Love,

Dad

Boys,

Discover what God wants you to do and follow it with your whole heart. I believe God gives us room to make choices along our way. He has your best interest at heart. Playing hard means giving life your best. Nothing less than your best is what God desires.

I've never told you to outscore someone, bring home trophies, or even win championships. But I require that you do your best. Whenever the school posts your report cards online, I ask one question: did you do your best? Don't think that you can trick me. Practice makes one have a good game, and I will know if you gave it your best by what you put into that.

Love,

Dad

Boys,

Jase, I cannot wait to discover what you want to do. Right now, you think you're Sonic Dash. Tyler once thought he was Superman. Knowledge and experience are what separates dreams from wisdom about God's plan for your lives.

I desire that you both complement and enhance any team you join. As you become team members, do your part with your whole heart. Contribute to the success of the group. Don't go solo or rogue. Remember that team chemistry is a work in progress. Simply put, be the person your team cannot live without. Be the one who is selfless with a work ethic that's inspiring.

Don't strive for titles. Instead, be the person who demonstrates the qualities of a loyal team member. It won't be easy to put others first, and I'm not saying allow others to run over you. I'm saying focus on serving Christ as you help others. That's the winning approach for life.

Some team members can and will be brutal. They'll be mean and do whatever it takes to succeed. Don't allow them to tear you down. Instead, ground yourself in Jesus, stay focused on the goal, and God will guide your success. When you arrive at a crossroads, choose wisely. Follow Jesus even if that path is less traveled.

Love,

Dad

Tyler and Jase,

Death comes to all. Your Permanent Score is the one that lasts forever. Your Permanent Score is settled here but enjoyed in heaven. You can't wait until heaven to check this box. God desires a lasting relationship with you both.

Tyler, I know you've settled your Permanent Score. My prayers are now for Jase. I'll walk patiently with him through that decision, as I did you, but if God calls me to heaven before then, please pick up where I leave off.

Don't fear life, difficulties, or death. As believers, we have won the war. Yes, we may lose a battle or two, but the victory is ours in Jesus.
Love,
Dad

Jase and Tyler,
You both know I would love to move to a remote wooded area where I could hunt and fish for the rest of my life. But can you imagine your mom living far away from a Target, Maggiano's, or Publix? Cathy, her hairstylist, would have to move with us! Ha-ha! Remote living is not on your mom's to-do list.

Seriously though, my hope when you two are grown is that your mom and I will always be available when you need us most. So go live your lives. Live them to the fullest while following Jesus. Dream big, follow your heart, be patient, and watch God do big things.
Love,
Dad

Tyler and Jase,
While my body might not be around, my heart and influence will always be with you because of my faith in Jesus. You might be thinking, "But, Dad, how will I know what you would say or do if you're not here"? The answer is simple: You'll know the right thing to do because you're my boys. Hopefully, I've modeled that life for you at home.

You'll know what to do because you've watched what I did when I needed help. I called out to Jesus and waited.

You've witnessed when others have mistreated us, and you watched as I went to Jesus and allowed Him to fight my battles. You also saw me love those who would harm me, not with my strength but with God's.

You've seen me on death's bed and listened as I asked God for a miracle.

You've been a part of situations when money got tight and saw how God showed up and showed out with His blessings.

You've seen when we needed something, and I taught you to pray and wait for His timing because He will provide.

You watched when I was unemployed and needed a job. I took what I could find to provide for our family.

You've heard me say, "Thank You."

You saw our family serve churches that needed help.

You went with me to the United Nations, and we walked to every country and prayed. We went to Washington, D.C., and walked to every embassy and prayed.

You've seen your mom and me love people right where they are with God's love.

That's how I know you'll know what to do when I'm not around. You've been able to observe us follow Jesus no matter what happened and no matter where He led us. I'm confident both of you will follow God's leading and that you'll also lead others to follow him.

If I'm not here physically, it's because I'm ahead of you on the journey. It means my Permanent Score was settled and recorded. And when my final whistle blew, I was ready.

When God calls me home, my work here will be over and my reward gifted. I'm not writing this letter for fear of leaving you but rather for the joy of seeing you reach and fulfill your Potential Scores. I cannot wait to see how God will use you in His plan.

Boys, have fun, laugh, learn, love, lead, and lean on Jesus. Life is short, so live it up. Teach my grandkids these first words: "Roll Tide!" And hold tightly to the promise of Psalm 91:1:

"The one who lives under the protection of the Most High dwells in the shadow of the Almighty."

Love,
Dad

A Note for My Readers

Fighting cancer while writing *Winning the Fatherhood Game* confirmed two things for me:

1. Absolutely nothing is impossible with God.
2. I really can do all things because He gives me strength!

I want you to absorb those truths into your soul too. They are grounded in life-affirming Scripture.

> *"Look, I am Yahweh, the God of all flesh. Is anything too difficult for me?"* (Jeremiah 32:27)

Wherever you are on your journey, and whatever your circumstances, God can do amazing things in your life—far greater things than you could ever imagine. That's a promise!

It has been an honor and privilege to mentor you man-to-man through this book. Now that you've developed a game plan for winning as a father, nothing should hold you back. You're ready to win! Grounded by your relationship with God, guided by the Holy Spirit, and bolstered by the camaraderie of other men, play the Fatherhood Game with your whole heart.

Let me add one more important thing: Memorizing Scripture is the best muscle-building exercise available for men who want to win the Fatherhood Game. When you commit Scripture to memory, it goes with you on the playing field, giving you wisdom for making calls and energizing you for the tough plays.

> *"All Scripture is inspired by God and is profitable for teaching, for rebuking, for correcting, for training in righteousness, so that the man of God may be complete, equipped for every good work."* (2 Timothy 3:16-17)

I've collected all the Bible verses featured in the book on the following pages for your easy access. Remove those pages (or photocopy them), so you can cut and post individual verses on your bathroom mirror, your car dash or gear shift, your desk—or wherever you'll see them every day. The inspired Word of God will empower you to leap the hurdles you encounter as a man and father.

I hope we meet someday on Earth so we can talk smack about football. *Roll Tide!* But if our paths never intersect on a field down here, I pray we'll meet in heaven one day because you were ready for your final whistle. You confirmed your Permanent Score by choosing victory in Jesus. And that made you a winner.

For the win,
Shannon
J. Shannon Eads

Muscle-Building Scriptures

"The one who lives under the protection of the Most High dwells in the shadow of the Almighty." (Psalm 91:1)

"You, therefore, my son, be strong in the grace that is in Christ Jesus. And what you have heard from me in the presence of many witnesses, commit to faithful men who will be able to teach others also." (2 Timothy 2:1-2)

"Also, if anyone competes as an athlete, he is not crowned unless he competes according to the rules." (2 Timothy 2:5)

"Not that I have already reached the goal or am already fully mature, but I make every effort to take hold of it because I also have been taken hold of by Christ Jesus. Brothers, I do not consider myself to have taken hold of it. But one thing I do: Forgetting what is behind and reaching forward to what is ahead, I pursue as my goal the prize promised by God's heavenly call in Christ Jesus." (Philippians 3:12-14)

"Whatever you do, do it enthusiastically, as something done for the Lord and not for men." (Colossians 3:23)

"Do not fear, for I am with you: do not be afraid, for I am your God. I will strengthen you; I will help you; I will hold on to you with my righteous right hand." (Isaiah 41:10)

"For you are saved by grace through faith, and this is not from yourselves; it is God's gift—not from works, so that no one can boast." (Ephesians 2:8-9)

"For God loved the world in this way: He gave His One and Only Son, so that everyone who believes in Him will not perish but have eternal life." (John 3:16)

"He will transform the body of our humble condition into the likeness of His glorious body, by the power that enables Him to subject everything to Himself." (Philippians 3:21)

"I am able to do all things through Him who strengthens me." (Philippians 4:13)

"For I know the plans I have for you," this is the Lord's declaration, *"plans for your welfare, not for disaster, to give you a future and a hope."* (Jeremiah 29:11)

"He has rescued us from the domain of darkness and transferred us into the kingdom of the Son He loves. We have redemption, the forgiveness of sins, in Him." (Colossians 1:13-14)

"Look, I am about to do something new; even now it is coming. Do you not see it? Indeed, I will make a way in the wilderness, rivers in the desert." (Isaiah 43:19)

"But you will receive power when the Holy Spirit has come on you, and you will be My witnesses in Jerusalem, in all Judea and Samaria, and to the ends of the earth." (Act 1:8)

"In the same way the Spirit also joins to help in our weakness, because we do not know what to pray for as we should, but the Spirit Himself intercedes for us with unspoken groanings. And He who searches the hearts knows the Spirit's mind-set, because He intercedes for the saints according to the will of God." (Romans 8: 26-27)

"*Be strong and courageous; don't be terrified or afraid of them. For it is the Lord your God who goes with you; He will not leave you or forsake you.*" (Deuteronomy 31:6)

"*Brothers, I do not consider myself to have taken hold of it. But one thing I do: Forgetting what is behind and reaching forward to what is ahead, I pursue as my goal the prize promised by God's heavenly call in Christ Jesus.*" (Philippians 3:13-14)

"*Search for the Lord and for His strength; seek His face always.*" (1 Chronicles 16:11)

"*I am sure of this, that He who started a good work in you will carry it on to completion until the day of Christ Jesus.*" (Philippians 1:6)

"*Finally brothers, whatever is true, whatever is honorable, whatever is just, whatever is pure, whatever is lovely, whatever is commendable—if there is any moral excellence and if there is any praise—dwell on these things. Do what you have learned and received and heard and seen in me, and the God of peace will be with you.*" (Philippians 4:8-9)

"*Therefore, my dear brothers, be steadfast, immovable, always excelling in the Lord's work, knowing that your labor in the Lord is not in vain.*" (1 Corinthians 15:58)

"*But those who trust in the Lord will renew their strength; they will soar on wings like eagles; they will run and not grow weary; they will walk and not faint.*" (Isaiah 40:31)

"*Now to Him who is able to do above and beyond all that we ask or think according to the power that works in us.*" (Ephesians 3:20)

"*Though an army deploys against me, my heart is not afraid; though a war breaks out against me, still I am confident.*" (Psalm 27:3)

"*Haven't I commanded you: be strong and courageous?* Do *not be be afraid or discouraged, for the* Lord *your* God *is with you wherever you go.*" (Joshua 1:9)

"*For the wages of sin is death, but the gift of* God *is eternal life in* Christ Jesus *our* Lord." (Romans 6:23)

"*For you are saved by grace through faith, and this is not from yourselves; it is* God's *gift—not from works, so that no one can boast.*" (Ephesians 2:8-9)

"*Look,* I *am* Yahweh, *the* God *of all flesh.* Is *anything too difficult for me?*" (Jeremiah 32:27)

"*For* God *loved the world in this way:* He *gave* His One *and* Only Son, *so that everyone who believes in* Him *will not perish but have eternal life.*" (John 3:16)

"*For everyone who calls on the name of the* Lord *will be saved.*" (Romans 10:13)

"*For me, living is* Christ *and dying is gain.*" (Philippians 1:21)

"*Just one thing:* Live *your life in a manner worthy of the gospel of* Christ. Then, *whether* I *come and see you or am absent, I will hear about you that you are standing firm in one spirit, with one mind, working side by side for the faith that comes from the gospel."* (Philippians 1:27)

"*Therefore, my dear brothers, be steadfast, immovable, always excelling in the Lord's work, knowing that your labor in the Lord is not in vain.*" (1 Corinthians 15:58)

"*Be alert, stand firm in the faith, act like a man, be strong.*" (1 Corinthians 16:13)

"*There is certainly no righteous man on the earth who does good and never sins.*" (Ecclesiastes 7:20)

"*Therefore, since we also have such a large cloud of witnesses surrounding us, let us lay aside every weight and the sin that so easily ensnares us. Let us run with endurance the race that lies before us.*" (Hebrews 12:1)

"*Do what you have learned and received and heard and seen in me, and the God of peace will be with you.*" (Philippians 4:9)

"*For all have sinned and fall short of the glory of God.*" (Romans 3:23)

"*Therefore, if anyone is in Christ, he is a new creation; old things have passed away, and look, new things have come.*" (2 Corinthians 5:17)

"*Go, therefore, and make disciples of all nations.*"(Matthew 28:19a)

"The one who walks with the wise will become wise, but a companion of fools will suffer harm." (Proverbs 13:20)

"Remember your leaders who have spoken God's word to you. As you carefully observe the outcome of their lives, imitate their faith." (Hebrews 13:7)

"Iron sharpens iron, and one man sharpens another." (Proverbs 27:17)

"Provide justice for the needy and the fatherless; uphold the rights of the oppressed and the destitute." (Psalm 82:3)

"And what you have heard from me in the presence of many witnesses, commit to faithful men who will be able to teach others also." (2 Timothy 2:2)

"He executes justice for the fatherless and the widow, and loves the foreigner, giving him food and clothing." (Deuteronomy 10:18)

"I will not leave you as orphans; I am coming to you." (John 14:18)

"Look, I am Yahweh, the God of all flesh. Is anything too difficult for me?" (Jeremiah 32:27)

"All Scripture is inspired by God and is profitable for teaching, for rebuking, for correcting, for training in righteousness, so that the man of God may be complete, equipped for every good work." (2 Timothy 3:16-17)

More Resources for Calling the Right Plays

There are many additional resources available to help you move forward. I've listed a few that can help you call the right plays during the Fatherhood Game. The men who wrote the following resources are some of the best coaches around. Their heads and hearts are in the game for you.

God Will Use This for Good by Max Lucado confirms that you can survive the messes of life and thrive.

Kingdom Man by Tony Evans goes into depth about how to deal with past issues that hamstring men.

Forward by David Jeremiah is packed with wisdom for getting unstuck.

The Purpose Driven Life by Rick Warren can help you create a game plan for pursuing your potential.

Winning the War of Your Mind by Craig Groeschel is a game-changer for rewiring your brain for success.

Make the Call by Mark Richt offers wisdom for life and leadership and encourages you to make the most important call of all.

Heaven by Randy Alcorn answers many questions about eternity and what awaits you as a child of God.

Deep Discipleship by J. T. English is a mentor's handbook.

Fields of the Fatherless by Tom Davis is an eye-opening guide for helping kids who need a father's wisdom and protection.

The Ministry for Men Website

Writing *Winning the Fatherhood Game* put me on the pitcher's mound. It felt great to throw that first pitch to men and get them in the game! Now I want to keep the ball moving.

God gave me a passion for helping churches, organizations, and businesses reach men with the gospel. I created the Ministry for Men website (www.ministryformen.com) as a one-stop coaching resource. It's packed with stories about everyday guys—both their triumphs and their struggles. You'll also find ministry tips and resources for building or strengthening a men's ministry, along with a gym bag full of game-changing equipment. There's some fun stuff in the bag too. After all, men need a good laugh to shake off the sweat of stress.

Strong men of faith are the special-teams players today's challenging world needs. I want to work with you to build a championship team of men. If your church doesn't have a ministry dedicated to men, or you want to know more about how *Ministry for Men* can help your church, organization, or business, let's connect soon. Together, we can be game-changers!

For the win,
J. Shannon Eads
shannon@ministryformen.com
www.ministryformen.com

Thank You

If you are thinking about writing a book and not sure where to begin, I would like to suggest these four businesses. They each made the process and path for me very doable. I could not have done it without their help and encouragement. Please consider using them in writing your book.

Ivey Harrington Beckman
Editor & Ghostwriter
Ivey Beckman Enterprises
www.iveyharringtonbeckman.com
iveyhb@gmail.com

Jess Rainer
Owner and Founder
Craft Book Publishing
www.craftbookpublishing.com
jess@craftbookpublishing.com

Ellen Lynch
Social Media
Ellen Lynch Design
www.ellenlynchdesigns.com
Ellen.royallynch@gmail.com

Christina Hinnant
Photography Blu LLC
www.photographyblullc.com
christina@photographyblullc.com

Endnotes

1 https://sportsspectrum.com/sport/football/2018/09/27/on-this-date-tim-tebow-delivers-emotional-promise-speech. Accessed September 29, 2021.

2 http://www.vincelombardi.com/quotes.html. Accessed May 6, 2021.

3 https://www.mensjournal.com/sports/13-athletes-who-made-amazing-comebacks-after-career-threatening-injuries/

4 https://twitter.com/CBSSports/status/1117496017337741312

5 https://www.mensjournal.com/sports/13-athletes-who-made-amazing-comebacks-after-career-threatening-injuries/

6 https://twitter.com/philmickelson/status/1392148755483303939 @ PhilMickelson

7 https://www.quotespedia.org/authors/w/winston-churchill/success-is-walking-from-failure-to-failure-with-no-loss-of-enthusiasm-winston-churchill/

8 Coaching U, CU [@Coaching_U]. (2016, December 15). "What happened yesterday is history. What happens tomorrow is a mystery. What we do today makes a difference." [Tweet]. Twitter. https://twitter.com/Coaching_U/status/809399411235233792

9 Andrew Weber, AW [@CoachAWeb]. (2021, April 1). "In the middle of difficulty lies opportunity." [Tweet]. Twitter. https://twitter.com/CoachAWeb/status/1377816128949518338

10 https://www.goalcast.com/2020/02/11/michael-jordan-quotes/

11 http://www.vincelombardi.com/quotes.html

12 Edwin Hernandez, EH [@EDWINIHERNANDE1]. (2017, January 4). "There may be people that have more talent than you. But there's no excuse for anyone to work harder than you do." [Tweet]. Twitter. https://twitter.com/EDWINIHERNANDE1

13 http://storiesoffaithandcourage.blogspot.com/2012/09/crippled-glenn-cunningham-became.html

14 http://storiesoffaithandcourage.blogspot.com/2012/09/crippled-glenn-cunningham-became.html
15 LamorInspiringStories https://www.youtube.com/watch?v=l7J7scxZGxs.
16 Norman Vincent Peale, The Amazing Results of Positive Thinking, Fireside, Simon & Schuster, New York, NY, 1959, 1987, 2003, p. 262.
17 https://www.reddit.com/r/GetMotivated/comments/2cgfyu/image_glenn_cunningham_us_olympian/
18 https://www.youtube.com/watch?v=9hIIUYVc3rE
19 https://www.youtube.com/watch?v=c_s2IbQ1Arg
20 https://www.baptistpress.com/resource-library/news/tony-dungy-voices-the-pain-lessons-from-his-sons-suicide/
21 https://www.baptistpress.com/resource-library/news/tony-dungy-voices-the-pain-lessons-from-his-sons-suicide/
22 "Faith, Football, and the Fervent Religious Culture at Dabo Swinney's Clemson" by Tim Rohan, Sports Illustrated NCAAF, September 23, 2019."
23 https://www.brainyquote.com/authors/dabo-swinney-quotes. Accessed July 7, 2021.
24 https://www.brainyquote.com/authors/dabo-swinney-quotes. Accessed July 7, 2021.
25 Dabo Swinney at the ACC Football Kickoff press conference July 18, 2018.
26 Dabo Swinney recorded at the ACC Football Kickoff press conference July 18, 2018.
27 https://www.baptistpress.com/resource-library/news/tony-dungy-voices-the-pain-lessons-from-his-sons-suicide/
28 https://www.allprodad.com/hope-for-the-future/accessed August 4, 2021.
29 https://www.mlb.com/news/pitchers-with-multiple-no-hitters
30 http://www.vincelombardi.com/quotes.html
31 Quoted in the movie Coach Carter, original to A Return to Love by Marianne Williamson, HarperPerennial, a division of Harper

Collins Publishers, New York, New York, 1992.
32 The Bowden Way, Bobby Bowden with Steve Bowden, Longstreet Press, Atlanta, GA 2001, page 81.
33 https://www.nytimes.com/2021/08/08/obituaries/bobby-bowden-dead.html
34 https://www1.cbn.com/sports/bobby-bowden%3A-a-legacy-of-coaching-champions-for-christ
35 https://www.news-journalonline.com/news/20180709/retired-coach-bobby-bowden-delivers-message-of-faith
36 http://kentuckytoday.staging.communityq.com/stories/hall-of-fame-coach-bobby-bowden-still-sharing-his-faith-to-the-world,13776?
37 https://www.boston.com/sports/sports-news/2021/08/14/bobby-bowden-remembered-faith-family-football/
38 https://fatherhoodfactor.com/us-fatherless-statistics/US Census Bureau, 2015] Living arrangements of children under 18 years and marital status of parents, by age, sex, race, and hispanic origin and selected characteristics of the child for all children: 2014. Washington, D.C.: U.S. Census Bureau.
39 Source: Allen, A. N., & Lo, C. C. (2012). Drugs, guns, and disadvantaged youths: Co-occurring behavior and the code of the street. Crime & Delinquency, 58(6), 932-953.

Made in the USA
Las Vegas, NV
04 December 2021

36115489R00073